TWO IN A RED CANOE
OUR JOURNEY DOWN THE YUKON

TEXT BY MEGAN BALDINO AND MATT HAGE

PHOTOGRAPHS BY MATT HAGE

FOREWORD BY BARBARA WASHBURN

GRAPHIC ARTS BOOKS

Lt. Frederick Schwatka was commissioned by the U.S. government
in 1883 to make a reconnaissance of the Yukon River from source to
mouth. Excerpts on pages 9, 53, 87, and 115 are drawn from his two-part
article, "The Great River of Alaska," which appeared in *The Century
Magazine* in 1885.

Excerpt on page 31 from *Yukon River (Dawson-Circle)* by Mike Rourke,
published by Rivers North Publications, Houston, B.C., 1996.

Library of Congress Cataloging-in-Publication Data

Baldino, Megan.
     Two in a red canoe : a summer on the yukon river / text by Megan
Baldino and Matt Hage ; photography by Matt Hage.
          p. cm.
     Includes bibliographical references (p.   )
     ISBN 1-55868-862-5 (softbound)
     1. Baldino, Megan—Travel—Yukon River (Yukon and Alaska)
2. Canoes and canoeing—Yukon River (Yukon and Alaska) 3. Yukon
River (Yukon and Alaska) — Description and travel. I. Title: 2 in a red
canoe. II. Hage, Matt. III. Title.
     F912.Y9B35 2005
     917.98'60452   2004012036

Graphic Arts Books
An imprint of Graphic Arts Center Publishing Company
P.O. Box 10306, Portland, Oregon 97296-0306
503-226-2402 / www.gacpc.com

PRESIDENT: Charles M. Hopkins
ASSOCIATE PUBLISHER: Douglas A. Pfeiffer
EDITORIAL STAFF: Timothy W. Frew, Tricia Brown, Jean Andrews,
     Kathy Howard, Jean Bond-Slaughter
PRODUCTION STAFF: Richard L. Owsiany, Heather Doornink,
     Vicki Knapton
EDITOR: George Bryson
DESIGNER: Elizabeth Watson
MAPMAKER: Marge Mueller, Gray Mouse Graphics
COVER PHOTOS: Front: The authors and their worthy craft, *Lucille*;
     Back: Where the river meets the Bering Sea at Emmonak, Alaska.
Pages 2-3: A June sunset over Kluane Lake, the largest in Canada's Yukon
     Territory. Page 5: A porcupine feeds on willows near Tanana, Alaska.

Printed and bound in the United States of America

For Matt, proof that anything is possible!
I love you.
— Megan

For Megan, a dream come true.
— Matt

ACKNOWLEDGMENTS

OUR MOST HEARTFELT thank you goes to Tricia Brown. Her guidance, encouragement, and leadership made this book a reality. Thank you! And to the rest of the team at Graphic Arts Center Publishing Company, especially George Bryson for his amazingly thorough and constructive edit.

Whether they were offering us advice, food, or a place to stay, the following people epitomize the spirit of the Yukon. May others be as lucky as we are to know you: Scott McDougall; Maria Van Bibber; John and Madeleine Gould; Adlai Alexander; Hannah Solomon and family; Cliff Adams and family; Jerry Thomas and Carol Pitka; Stan Zuray and family; Charlie Campbell and Ruth Althoff; David and Patty Bowen; Randy Shaw and Lucy Williamson; John Stam; Lucy Whalen; Walter Stickman; Wilfred Deacon; Shawn Ingalls; Len and Jeanie Fabich. And to all those who let us intrude, thank you.

We are so grateful to our families for supporting our journey, no matter how crazy they thought it was. Lacy and William Leigh, thanks for dropping us off and shipping our food; Carol Casey, thanks for picking us up. Thanks also to Marilou Baldino, Dan Baldino, Lucille Pierson, and the entire Baldino family, who spent the summer of 2001 praying for our safe return, as well as Larry and Leona Hage.

We want to thank those who supported our journey before we even left: Charlene Marth of Doyon Native Corporation; Annette Freiburger, who was leading the Fairbanks Native Association; and Patricia Watts and Kelly Bostian at the *Fairbanks Daily News-Miner*. Also to Roy Corral, thanks for all the advice.

And finally to *Lucille*, for holding us together when we were falling apart!

CONTENTS

ANOTHER PARTNERSHIP FORGED IN THE WILDERNESS

By Barbara Washburn

It is a privilege for me to salute Megan Baldino and Matt Hage, two people who have shared adventure in Alaska, as my mountain-climbing husband and I did many years ago. The only difference is that I had just married Brad and had to appear courageous in front of other expedition members. Megan and Matt were still courting when they made this epic journey, yet it is no surprise that they married only three months later. Sharing extended time in the wilderness tends to seal a partnership for good.

Their experiences are fascinating, from battling whitecaps on Lake Laberge at the beginning of the trip, to slogging through the lower Yukon's mudflats near the Bering Sea. One day they set up camp in Anvik on the lawn of the beautiful log church where Olie and Mardy Murie were married in 1924. Brad and I remember meeting the Muries in McKinley Park in the 1940s. They were living their Alaska dream, with Mardy assisting her husband in his work as a biologist. She would go on to write about those exciting years of their early married life in *Two in the Far North*.

And now in *Two in a Red Canoe*, Matt and Megan represent the next generation of adventurer couples,

and I admire Megan tremendously for helping Matt fulfill his dream. I especially enjoyed her remarks, "If my friends could see me now!" I recalled when I had to relieve myself on the summit of 10,000-foot Mount Bertha. There was no bush to hide behind, but Brad said "No problem," and he tied a rope around my waist and let me down a steep slope, out of sight of our companions. As I looked out from that huge height toward the ocean, I giggled and said to myself, "If my friends could see me now!"

This was a suspenseful book for me, because I wanted so badly to have Matt achieve his goal. And yet, I also saw in many ways reaching the mouth of the Yukon River was less important than what these two discovered along the way—about each other and about the river and its people. In that regard, the journey was a success for both of them. I congratulate them and wish them many more adventures.

———

In 1947, Barbara Washburn became the first woman to reach the summit of Mount McKinley. She is married to the famed mountaineer, photographer, and mapmaker Bradford Washburn, and is the author of The Accidental Adventurer.

Megan and Matt pause for a photo at the United States–Canada border.

PART I

YOUCON

LAKE LABERGE, YUKON TERRITORY, TO CIRCLE, ALASKA

*Why this route had not been picked out long ago by some explorer, who
could thereby traverse the whole river in a single summer instead of
combating its swift current from its mouth, seems singular, and can only
be explained by supposing that those who would place sufficient reliance
on the Indian reports to put in their maps the gross inaccuracies that fill
even all our Government charts of the Yukon's source, would be very likely
to place reliance on the same Indians; and these, from time immemorial,
have united in pronouncing this part of the river unnavigable even by
canoes, filled as it is with rapids, whirlpools, and cascades.*

— Lt. Frederick Schwatka, 1883

TO ME ALASKA has always been a place where the impossible seems
possible. There is a reason they call it the Last Frontier; dreams
materialize in the strangest places when people least expect them. My
dream was a simple one: land a job in broadcast journalism. At the time
the only TV station that would hire me was in Fairbanks, one of the
smallest markets in the country. I knew nothing about Alaska and
planned on staying just long enough to get another resumé tape together.
After just a few weeks, those plans changed drastically. I was falling in

*Lake Laberge, a 30-mile-long reservoir for the Yukon River,
offered a key link to water transportation during the 1898 Klondike gold rush
and a historical starting point for many adventures in the last 150 years.*

9

Matt pilots Lucille *from the stern on the Thirtymile River. Brimmed hats, bandanas, and glasses protect us from the intense sun on the water.*

love with the state and a man named Matt. In what seemed like an instant, my life changed forever.

Matt was unlike any other person I had ever met. He was raised in Alaska and had never lived anywhere else. He climbed mountains and had recently reached the top of Denali, the tallest peak in North America. Matt ran marathons and participated in 50-kilometer ski races. His home was a small log cabin without running water. Not out of necessity, but simplicity. On the weekends he would read while listening to public radio and at night take me to the symphony at the university. He, too, is a journalist and was working as a photographer for the *Fairbanks Daily News-Miner.* We met on assignment just days after my arrival in Fairbanks. Journalism was the one thing we had in common, otherwise we were complete opposites. I grew up in the northern suburbs of Chicago. If Matt was small town, I was most definitely uptown. I liked expensive restaurants, brand-name clothing, and running water. So, I don't know how it happened, but it did. I fell instantly in love with his charming manners, handsome looks, and outlandish sense of adventure. Maybe I fell too hard. Just two months after we started dating, we started planning. Not a wedding—but a 2,000-mile journey down the Yukon River from Canada to the Bering Sea. The impossible had just become possible for me.

The idea of floating the Yukon River with each other sounded magical, and the dark, cold days of winter are the perfect time to plan a summer trip. Days after hatching our plan, we pored through every book we could find on the Yukon. Historical photographs revealed haggard prospectors, Natives, and a country untamed by man. A journey downriver would take us through a land first known by wandering Athabascan Indians and Yup'ik Eskimos and later explored by Hudson's Bay Company fur trappers and Russian traders. Their outposts of Fort Yukon, Nulato, and Saint Marys still stand on the river's banks as a vestige of the first settlements. Those first explorers named the waterway Youcon, or the Great River. The river's reputation lives up to its name. It is the third-largest river in North America, and drains 330,000 square miles of British Columbia, Yukon Territory, and Alaska.

Many pictures we looked at showed a difficult life in a harsh land. Crossing the famous Chilkoot Trail in winter did not look inviting, nor did poling a boat in summer. Yet so many pictures depicted the romance of the river. One of my favorites showed a group of well-dressed men and women dancing on the deck of a sternwheeler. Decorations draped the outdoor patio enclosed with several small trees. A band played music from the side. Travel on the river back then was sometimes a grand social occasion.

Megan checks the gargantuan grocery list. To prepare, we sorted 90 days' worth of groceries in our cabin outside Fairbanks. Supplies were boxed and shipped out to villages for pickup during our voyage.

Realizing a dream is an amazing, overwhelming feeling. I put my broadcasting career on hold for this trip. I know this will be a trip Matt and I will share like no other. I could not spend six weeks on a mountain with him; it just isn't in my blood. But this I can do, and that makes it even more special.

— Megan

Loaded to the gunwales, Lucille and Megan sit ready to put in at Policeman's Point at the head of Lake Laberge.

"If they can do it, I can do it," I told Matt one day.

"Of course you can do it," he responded.

I loved his confidence in me. I didn't know then that it would carry me through many days on our summerlong journey.

For such a grand voyage we were going to need the perfect craft. Matt and I combed the newspapers, hunted out "For Sale" signs, and shopped outdoor retailers. Matt was excited to find a deal on a 1960s-era Folbot, a wooden-framed collapsible kayak made for two.

"I'm not riding in a Fol-nothing," I replied to his idea that we float 2,000 miles in this rickety old boat. Luck hit when we least expected it, in the middle of winter. The January classified ad simply read "18-foot Old Town canoe, $500." When we arrived she was upside down on sawhorses, her red hull poking out under a thick blanket of snow. With an indestructible underbelly and room for over 1,000 pounds of cargo, she was the one. Still, it was a risky buy; all the open water was frozen solid and we wouldn't know how she floated until May.

Her name came easy. We decided she would be christened after many strong and stubborn women in my family, including my grandmother.

"*Lucille* it is," Matt had said. He was so proud the day he painted her name in white on her bow.

The smile on his face that day is the one I see today as we pack the boat, a grin of excitement and accomplishment.

"Meg, hand me the fishing rods," Matt says as he packs them into the back of the canoe. I hand him the two poles and look around suddenly, realizing that more than 800 pounds of gear is tucked into *Lucille*. My heart thumps in my chest as I glance at the boat just inches from the water.

"Can you believe we are finally here?" he asks. I ponder the question, thinking back to the long distance we have already traveled. It was a road paved with challenges, doubts, laughs, and, most importantly, love. I look at Matt and notice the twinkle in his eyes. Floating the Yukon is not just another adventure for him. Today he begins a lifetime dream—to photograph the people and places along the river—and I am his partner. I feel absolutely honored.

"All right, ready to go?" Matt says with a huge smile on his face.

"Let's do it!" I say, and with that we climb into *Lucille* and start paddling.

On Lake Laberge, four hours into the first day of paddling.

"Isn't it great, Meg? Look how calm the water is." Matt is paddling like a pro. Each stroke a passionate move toward his goal. I follow his lead and soon *Lucille's* awkward wobble evens out. I take a cautious look around, not fully believing that I am in the wilds of the fabled Yukon Territory, Canada. We are surrounded by beauty just minutes into the trip. At the head of Lake Laberge, the other end is not visible, but on each side of us lie freshly greened valleys, limestone rock outcrops, and gravel shorelines. The quiet shocks me into my own silence. I dip my hand in the water.

"It's freezing," I say.

"Yeah," Matt says, "the ice probably just gave out last week." I look at my watch, the date reads June 9.

IT WAS THE SUMMER of 1898, the height of the Klondike gold rush, and the stubborn sheet of ice covering Lake Laberge was holding up the whole show. An anxious horde, numbering in the thousands, had traveled over the Chilkoot Pass that winter, bypassing the already crowded shores of Lake Bennett to set up shop on Laberge. By putting in the extra 100 miles, the prospectors hoped to beat most of the 30,000 other stampeders bound for the goldfields. They worked on the banks through the spring, whipsawing green lumber and building a ragtag fleet of simple craft to carry them more than 400 miles to Dawson City. The ice on the Yukon had already gone out, but the lakes remained locked tight.

The gold rush of the late 19th century put Laberge on the map, and its status as a major landmark on the trail to the Klondike made it a household name around the globe. Before then, this 30-mile reservoir to the Yukon River was just one of hundreds of lakes gathering water in northwestern Canada. No roads led to its isolated shores. Ocean-borne shipping extended only to the lower Yukon, hundreds of miles away. Anticipating the coming onslaught of gold-seekers, the Royal Canadian Mounted Police established two outposts on the lake to maintain order: one at the head, today called Policeman's Point, and one at the lower end where it empties into the Thirtymile River. River pilots were required to check in at both posts before continuing.

That year the ice finally broke on May 29, opening the door to the Yukon for more than 7,000 handmade craft. A haphazard armada of hastily built boats scurried

June 9
Lake Laberge,
Yukon Territory

We have arrived!
The infamous Lake
Laberge. It was very
exciting to push off into
the water after a full
year of planning this
expedition. Ended up
way out in the lake
when the afternoon
wind picked up. We
scurried for the shore in
a panic. Good wake-up
call. Paddled for another
hour to make camp on a
rocky point.
                    —Matt

Paddlers make their way along the craggy shores of Lake Laberge.

June 11

Today the color of Lake Laberge was crystal-clear aquamarine. It was stunning. We saw an eagle and moved in. I was literally about 10 feet from it before it flew away. The lake is unreal and so uninhabited. There is nothing out here, but the trees whistling and the waves lapping into shore. We have seen maybe six planes in three days. Tomorrow we hit the Thirtymile [River].

— Megan

to the lake's outlet and into the Yukon River. Within two days, the city of tents that once crowded the shores of Laberge was gone.

The 500-mile race to the goldfields along the Klondike River, a tributary of the Yukon, was on. But for many it was short-lived. Stormy weather swamped poorly loaded boats, and those of questionable construction sank outright. Hundreds were left stranded after the shallow rapids of the Thirtymile River destroyed their craft. The river's bends became traffic jams as naïve oarsmen piled up on the deviously submerged boulders and hard-to-avoid sandbars.

As I BEGIN to ponder the strange empty feeling settling in, a light wind pushes *Lucille* sideways a bit and catches my attention. The advice of an outfitter in Whitehorse rings in my ears: *If the wind picks up, get off the lake.* Before we know it the glassy water of Lake Laberge suddenly changes to a torrent of waves. Matt and I look at each other with concern. "Just paddle!" I shout. We quickly turn the canoe and pull furiously for shore.

This is the Lake Laberge we have heard so much about—quick winds, furious waves, and whitecaps warning of danger. It's only the first hour of our trip and doubt shudders from our shoulders through every stroke of the paddles.

We had bought top-of-the-line life jackets. I look down to make sure mine is fastened tight. I notice the thick black fanny pack around my waist. Matt is wearing one as well. Inside we had placed items we would need in case of an emergency. Waterproof matches, lighters, gas, a compass, a whistle, a reflector, and some non-perishable food. We had agreed the fanny packs would remain on our waists whenever we were in the boat. At first it felt very uncomfortable, but now as the water shakes the boat, I'm happy it's around my waist.

I had wondered before the trip if I was prepared for the danger of traveling in such remote wilderness. If anything happened there would seldom be any way to get help. The thought makes me paddle hard as the water works itself into a frenzy. Ten minutes later, the adrenaline still pumping through our hearts, we make it to the gravel shore.

"Beginner's luck," Matt laughs.

CAMP THAT NIGHT is a rocky beach. Matt has wandered off with his camera, leaving me to get dinner going. Alone on the beach, I feel like I may as well be on Mars. Our gear is spread out in no particular order. I reach for the tent and spend five minutes trying to get it out of its bag. More doubts flood my brain as I fumble with the poles and stakes. I have been camping with Matt dozens of times, but this time feels different.

One of our first dates was a 12-mile uphill ski to a remote cabin in interior Alaska. I had only been skiing a few times, and the trip was a big challenge. In the end, I finished and even managed to cook a meal. It wasn't that I wanted to impress Matt, but I wanted us to enjoy the outing as much as I knew he wanted me to enjoy it. At the end of the ski trip, he was proud of me because he understood I was out of my element and had met the challenge. Later I would show him the same courtesy at my sister's wedding when he had to wear a new shirt and tie and sit at the head table.

High winds suddenly turned the glassy waters of Lake Laberge into a rolling sea of whitecaps. Megan checks our progress on the map while we wait out the afternoon winds.

A woodstove in the old telegraph station remains at the site of an 1899 Royal North-West Mounted Police post at Lower Laberge. Several other buildings in the area include a barracks, post office, and roadhouse. The ghost town marks the end of the 30-mile-long lake at the mouth of the Thirtymile River.

The trip down the Yukon was different from the ski trip, though. From the beginning we worked as a team, planning every detail of the journey. As we mapped it all out, our relationship grew stronger. Matt thought of all the little things to make the trip less daunting and more comfortable for me once we were on the river.

"Variety will make all the difference," he kept saying. "We need plenty of different types of food and some card games." He suggested things like a solar shower, a thick sleeping pad, a portable CD player. It's strange to see all of the items finally out here. Feeling a little overwhelmed, I grab the CD player and put in some Bob Dylan. Matt's plan works. I feel better already.

As I boil water for pasta and butter some bread, I hear the shutter on his camera. I look up from the stove and see the beautiful sunset that has captured his attention. The flat water of Laberge reflects a mirror image of the sky. Tremendous white clouds break up the purple and orange sunset. A loon sits on the surface of the water bellowing to its partner. I am stunned by the beauty and look back at Matt. He smiles reassuringly. Loving Matt is so easy, and tonight fills me with a sense of peace absent during the last week's pretrip stress. It was exactly what we hoped for, a picture-perfect moment the first night of our trip. I stop doubting and start enjoying. As I listen to the camera's shutter and the loons in the distance, I remember why I am here and secretly hope every night is as good as this.

We decide to remain close to shore as we travel Lake Laberge the next day. Matt sits in the back of the boat guiding *Lucille*. As the morning sun deepens, the water changes from hazy blue to a deep azure color. There are no motorboats and no airplanes. It's the most serene silence I've ever experienced. An Arctic tern dances in the sky above us, periodically making a sudden dive for food. Farther down the lake a bald eagle sits on top of a spruce tree. We get within 20 feet of the enormous bird and it never makes a move.

Signs of the gold rush also line the lake's shore. At the mouth of the Thirtymile, a deserted mining camp is still largely intact. The skeletal hull of the steamship *Casca I* lies scattered in ruins on the beach. What was once a large steamship carrying supplies and passengers from Whitehorse to Dawson is now just a few pieces of wood. It's another reminder that we are not the first inexperienced travelers to come this way. I think about the prospectors. I wonder: Were they as naïve as I? Did they know how raw the silence would be? Or how far the landscape would stretch?

As I look at the few dozen pieces of wood scattered on the beach, it's obvious that what's left of the *Casca*—and many other items at the mouth of the Thirtymile—will soon disappear entirely.

THE FIRST STEAMBOAT to ply the Yukon's waters was the nearly 50-foot-long *Youkon*, built in 1869. Operated by the Alaska Commercial Company, the crew piloted her on a 27-day expedition through uncharted waters from the old Russian port of St. Michael in Norton Sound on Alaska's west coast, to the trading post at Fort Yukon, more than a thousand miles upriver. This maiden voyage opened up the wide, deep channels of the lower and middle Yukon to steamship traffic. During the 1800s, most trade from the Yukon drainage came down the river and connected with oceangoing vessels at St. Michael.

Transportation companies wasted no time in expanding their service on the Yukon, building a fleet of flagship stern-wheelers such as the 140-foot *Bella*, the 160-foot *Alice*, and the 175-foot *Portus B. Weare*. But it was the Alaska Commercial Company that rose to the occasion and landed its 140-foot *Arctic* in Dawson City in 1897.

June 13
Thirtymile River,
Yukon Territory

Our camp at US Bend is very fine. The river's clear aquamarine currents flow by as we have breakfast and the picnic table is a real plus. . . . Meg pulled two grayling out of the river last night, which we promptly grilled over a fire for our dinner. The larger of the two was a meal in itself. The Thirtymile swiftly drains Lake Laberge and collides with the silty water of the Teslin River up ahead. This is where the Yukon starts its life as a major waterway. I'll be happy to be on the Yukon proper, but will miss the sassy, clear water of the Thirtymile.
　　　　　—Matt

The Thirtymile River drains Lake Laberge into the mighty Yukon. Shallow depths, numerous riffles, and tight bends brought havoc to stern-wheeler captains of a century ago.

Communities up and down the 2,000-mile-long river began to depend on the commerce brought in aboard the stern-wheelers. Their decks were filled with food supplies, tools for prospectors, and whiskey from the outside heading upriver. A wealth of rough gold, furs, and passengers crowded aboard for the trip out. With its shallow flats and switching channels, the Yukon presented a difficult challenge for the river pilots. Steamers spent days stranded after running onto submerged sandbars. On its first trip to supply the mining town of Fortymile, near the Alaska–Canada border, the *Arctic* was wrecked 1,600 miles from the settlement and unable to continue.

The ACC sent runners to relay an urgent message to the miners waiting at Fortymile for their winter rations: get out of the Yukon before freeze-up or risk starving. The *New Racket* was dispatched to rescue the prospectors, arriving just as the October snow began to fall. The community was evacuated, packed like sardines on the little stern-wheeler bound for St. Michael. It ran too late and was frozen solid on the river nearly two hundred miles from port, which the passengers covered on foot at a heavy price.

The gold rush attracted a steady run of stern-wheelers to the upper Yukon Basin. An engineer from Iowa, A. J. Goddard, and his wife packed two disassembled stern-wheelers over the Chilkoot Pass. They rebuilt the vessels on Lake Bennett and offered the first steamboat service from the Yukon's headwaters. Only the larger ship, *Bellingham*, made it to Dawson, as the second went down in a storm on Lake Laberge near the outlet to the Thirtymile. Steamers began to make the run from Whitehorse downriver to Dawson City, where they encountered a much narrower winding waterway than what lay ahead on the vast mile-wide channel in western Alaska. The Thirtymile, a small section of the Yukon that drains Lake Laberge to meet the Teslin River, took its toll on early shipping traffic. Numerous landmarks along its swift riffles and tight bends memorialize the dramas that played out here: Casca Reef, La France Creek, and Domeville Bar all mark the wrecks of their respective stern-wheelers.

The popularity of railroads, and later highways, slowly brought the demise of the shipping business on the Yukon. Though the remoteness of Alaska and northwest Canada helped extend the life of the stern-wheeler, by the mid-1920s only nine ran the upper river, and the *Yukon* was alone on the Alaska side. The last steamer built on the Yukon was the *Klondike 2* in 1937, when the remaining stern-wheelers were contracted to help haul materials for the construction of the Alaska Highway, a project that brought a final end to their service.

The *Whitehorse* was the last working stern-wheeler to churn the Yukon in 1952. Today the *Keno* sits on display in Dawson City and the *Klondike* is preserved in Whitehorse for all to see. The hulls of the *Bella* and the larger *Portus B. Weare* sit rotting in St. Michael in Norton Sound.

THE THIRTYMILE RIVER is crystal clear and its narrow channels are a nice change from Lake Laberge. It is early in the season and the water is high, making travel quick and exciting. Tall green fir trees line the shore, sometimes dropping into the water, sometimes giving way to a rocky beach. Amazing sand sculptures formed by the wind jut out from several cliffs. The Thirtymile is every bit as beautiful as we've been told. We had been unsuccessful in catching any fish on Laberge, but the Thirtymile is generous and each night we feast on fresh grayling.

After five days it finally happens: we turn a small bend and float into the Yukon.

"It looks filthy," I tell Matt.

"Silt," he says. "Listen carefully and you can hear it on the bottom of the boat."

June 14

Matt is tired so I cook for him. He seems to have acquired an accent, that of a cowboy. He is in heaven, talking like this is the only land and life he's ever known. How will I keep up with him?
— Megan

The sound was a welcome change from the intense quiet of the last week. The shape of the water also intrigued me. Massive boils circulate on the river's surface and look as if they will suck us into the murky water.

My mom's words echo in my ears: "You're never coming home."

I smile at the thought of my mother in Chicago, so very, very far away. I suddenly feel homesick. My family was taking a "once-in-a lifetime" trip to Tuscany this summer. The trip materialized just weeks after I committed to the Yukon, our own "once-in-a-lifetime" trip. We anticipated our adventure was going to take three

months. That meant not only was Italy out, but also my annual summer trip to Chicago. It was a tough decision for me. Being so far from my family is the one thing that makes my decision to stay in Alaska so difficult. If it wasn't for Matt, I might be working at a small television station somewhere in Illinois.

"Hey Meg, look at the two rivers melding together," Matt says getting my attention. I glance down and notice the change. *So different, so alike, kind of like Matt and me.* I turn around and look at my partner for the first time on the Yukon River and realize how happy I am that I don't work at a small television station somewhere in Illinois.

Megan washes her hair in the clear waters of the Thirtymile River.

We plan to camp at Hootalinqua, where the Thirtymile merges with the silty waters of the Teslin. The junction forms the main body of the Yukon River. What was once an outpost for the Royal Canadian Mounted Police is today a riverside campground maintained by Parks Canada. New picnic tables and an outhouse mix with the ruins of Klondike-era cabins. We tie up the canoe and scout out possible tent sites, my eyes focused on the ground while I scan for signs of bear. Suddenly, a heavy growl breaks the silence of the river and the blood drains from my face. Eyes wide, I slowly back-step to the canoe. I scan the tree line, but don't see anything threatening. Regardless, my heart is in my throat and my legs are shaking. Matt tries to convince me everything is all right, but looks uncertain as he also makes a move for our boat. The mysterious roar came from over near the outhouse and sounded like a large animal either breathing loudly or grunting. Petrified of being mauled, my body is frozen in the back of the canoe, paddle in hand.

"Let's get out of here," I whisper sternly. Matt hesitates for a second before pushing us off into the current. We sit just offshore, waiting to catch a glimpse of the unknown predator.

"I don't think it's a bear," he says tentatively. "It was probably a door or something." My mind is made up, with or without Matt I am leaving. He turns around and starts to say something, but one look at my face and he starts to paddle us downriver in search of the next camp spot.

Just a few minutes later, *Lucille*'s hull skids onto the sandy shores of Shipyard Island. There is a flat clearing for our tent just below the hulking remains of the steamship *Evelyn*, left to rot here by the Northern Commercial Company in the early 1930s. The entire island was used as a dry dock for boats on the Yukon River. Beams of weathered lumber lay scattered in the willows with rusty cast-iron tools of industry. Oversized pulleys and cables tell us how they towed the giant vessels onto the beach.

Once so full of life, it's amazing just how empty the deserted stern-wheeler makes me feel. Trees have grown over much of the boat, but its menacing shadow peers over us as we set up camp. This site is no more comforting than the last one, and I search the perimeter for paw prints. My bear paranoia is getting out of control. I had not expected to be so terrified of something we have not even seen yet, but I am.

The remains of the steamship Evelyn *rest on Shipyard Island just below the junction with the Teslin River. She was built in Seattle in 1908, wrecked on the Tanana River in 1913, and retired here in 1930.*

June 17, Sunday
Carmacks, Yukon Territory

A double truss bridge spans the Yukon River here. Its steel girders connect the small town of Carmacks with the Indian village on the north banks. All day villagers make the crossing to the town; no one from town goes to the village. It is a strange structure that gives villagers access to the white man's world, but not a connection.
—Matt

A ground squirrel sentinel watches over his claim at the abandoned telegraph post in the gold rush town of Big Salmon, Yukon Territory. Prospectors started showing up in the village known as Ta-Tlin-Hini, or Big Salmon, during the 1880s.

Sleep does not come easy. I begin to dread the moment I have to close my eyes and let my guard down. I am convinced that as soon as I fall asleep a bear will pounce on our tent and eat me alive. Matt, sensing my exhaustion and fear, reassures me over and over that this is a safe campsite. Still, I scan the tree line for predators with eyes wide. Matt says I look like a doe caught in the headlights of an oncoming truck as I continually watch over my shoulder. He fixes us dinner and urges me to get some sleep.

In the morning a layer of fog hangs over the Yukon. The air is damp and chilly, the river peaceful and quiet. I'm still a little down; neither of us slept well, as we woke to check out every little noise. We sit on the banks of the Yukon with a hot breakfast of oatmeal and strong coffee, when another boat emerges silently from the mist. We haven't seen anyone for a week and company is exactly what I need. Margaret Moreau and Manfred Kuchenmuller slide their beat-up white canoe onto the beach. I offer them a cup of coffee as we introduce ourselves. Both have long graying hair that hangs down to their plastic rain ponchos. Margaret takes in our comfortable camp, including our French coffee press, with clinical precision behind fogged-up

One of only three bridges spanning the Yukon River connects the truck-stop town of Carmacks with the Native village of the same name. Both are named after George Carmack, who is said to have built a collection of cabins in the area.

glasses. She says nothing as she mouses around with her hands clenched behind her. Manfred wastes no time in getting to the point. He tells us they are both psychologists from Vancouver, British Columbia, and this is their second run of the Yukon.

"You have to move fast or you won't make it to the Bering Sea," warns Manfred. The couple paddled as far as the village of Kaltag, about a thousand miles from here, on their previous Yukon trip. By that August the weather was so awful, they decided to get off the river. Manfred preaches a doctrine of "light is right" and shows us a large plastic bin of dried soup mix. This is what they have brought to eat for the entire 2,000-mile journey. Breakfast, lunch, and dinner. "You just dip your cup in and add hot water," he says proudly. "It's easy." From across the beach Margaret chimes in with a groan, clearly tired of their mono-meal.

Later that afternoon, feeling better, Matt and I talk about the possibility of not making it all the way to the Bering Sea. With three months' travel time, we figured it would be no problem, but Manfred's warning got us thinking.

"Maybe we have too much stuff," I say looking around the canoe.

"We're fine," Matt says, "half the stuff in here is equipment. We are going to make it."

I grab a tube of Pringles and eat half of it. *Poor Margaret*, I think to myself.

AFTER A MONTHLONG JOURNEY from the Norton Sound port of St. Michael, the *Excelsior* steamed into San Francisco loaded with gold and the crazed faces of miners fresh from the Klondike. The July 14, 1897, homecoming brought substance to the rumors circulating around a nation idling in economic depression. With the help of the nation's largest newspapers, the hype of the Klondike spread like wildfire through an impoverished America. Soon it seemed as if the entire Western world was pointing to a theretofore unknown river in northwestern Canada. About 40 different nationalities of prospectors were represented to some extent in the Klondike stampede: Japanese, Chinese, Finns, Swedes, Germans, Poles, Brits, Irish, and Scots came in great numbers searching for gold. There were Russian Jews and French Canadians working side by side to mine a claim. An estimated 100,000 men and women joined in the rush to the Yukon with hopes to dig their own fortunes.

The Klondike gold rush was one of the greatest adventures ever to take place in North America. Over a century later, travelers from around the world come to the Yukon River to dip their toes in the currents of history or take a ride through some famed wilderness. Parks Canada registers about 1,500 people for the 467-mile river trip from Whitehorse to Dawson City every summer. During our Yukon journey we would paddle with New Zealanders, share campfire corn bread with German police officers, and enjoy a cold beer with a Swiss trio on a sandbar in the middle of a mile-wide river. Like us, they have come to travel on this world-famous waterway simply because it's the Yukon: a perfect balance of wild beauty, cultural history, and wilderness challenges. One German traveler summed it up best: "There's no other place like this in the world."

IT HAPPENS QUICKLY. The mosquitoes attack without warning and without mercy. They swarm us in the thousands whenever we reach shore. At Big Salmon Village they are awful. "Spray up!" Matt says. He grabs the bug spray and some DEET and douses his entire body. He sprays it in his ears, all over his face, and under and on his clothes. I look on pondering the prospect of using that much bug spray without a shower to rinse off that night. I smack my ear, but the buzzing is incessant.

"Use a lot or you'll be sorry," my loving partner says.

"I'll risk it," I say, using a fraction of the spray. It doesn't take long before I learn my lesson. The bugs are everywhere and crawling into any and every open crevice of my clothes. I look at Matt; despite all the bug spray, thousands of mosquitoes are clutching his purple fleece jacket. I look at the 20 bites on my arms, then back at Matt and take a bath in DEET. I grab my head net and put that on as well, but not before spitting out a few mosquitoes.

Tired, hungry, and dirty, I am thrilled when the Klondike Highway Bridge finally comes into view. The only span over the Yukon between Whitehorse and Dawson City, it marks the small truck-stop town of Carmacks. I haven't showered in a week and the dusty streets are a welcome sight. We pull into a small, deserted riverside campground and set up camp. The only community we've seen in a week,

Spinning aimlessly in the current, Joe and Aaron Brillhart kick back on their way to Carmacks. The father-and-son team from Pennsylvania spent two weeks on the popular float trip from Whitehorse to Dawson City.

we have a long list of chores, including recharging batteries for the video camera, laundry, showering, and calling home.

Matt and I call home just in time for Father's Day. Although he does not say it, my dad is relieved to hear from us. He is worried and asks me to call more often. I try to explain what it's like out on the Yukon, but he is in Chicago and does not fully understand how hard it is to find a phone along this stretch of the river. I linger for a few more minutes, not wanting to hang up. The next phone call will have to wait until Dawson City, about a week away. Finally the thought of a shower pulls me away. It's been over a week and there is a thick film on my skin. I haven't touched my hair

The stern-wheeler Whitehorse
negotiates the notorious
Five Finger Rapids.
[Photo by Case & Draper: Alaska
State Library PCA #39-56]

in two days. Instead I stuff it under a baseball cap. If my friends and coworkers at the TV station could see me now! I actually do not mind the dirt. It's nice not having to think about my appearance on a daily basis. Besides, I have bigger things to worry about: tomorrow we run through Five Finger Rapids, the only patch of whitewater on the entire Yukon River.

FOR THE 3,000 STAMPEDERS who floated from Lake Bennett to Dawson City, the rapids at Five Fingers presented a deadly obstacle. Homemade boats were reduced to splinters in the powerful waters. In his river guidebook to the Yukon, author Mike Rourke included a particularly harrowing account from 1898 by Czech prospector Jan Welzl:

> *Beyond these dangerous rapids there was a small police station on the shore, and near it a special sort of net was stretched across the river so that all the people who were drowned could be caught in it and their identity established. The water is very rough for a distance of about a mile before reaching this net, and we were constantly tossed up and down. If anyone manages to get safely past this spot at the moment when they have taken any corpses out of the water each gold miner has to dig a grave and bury one corpse on a small hill near by. For this work, which was compulsory, he receives ten dollars.*

THE RIVER IS DIVIDED into five turbulent channels at the rapids by large granite bluffs, hence Five Finger Rapids. We pull into a small side eddy to scope out our route. It looks much worse than we imagined. I scan the surface and cringe at the sight of three- to four-foot standing waves. We've been advised to run through the right-hand channel, but today it's a torrent of powerful crosscurrents. The only choice is to take the waves head-on. A 100-foot-long tree floats quickly by in the Yukon's current and we watch it as if it's our test dummy. After it disappears in the foaming rapids, our nerves go into high gear and we paddle into the current.

I look to either side of the river for a place to swim, just in case we go over. We are both wearing our life jackets and fanny packs. The sound is deafening as we

June 19, Tuesday
Minto, Yukon Territory

Yesterday was the day
that I piloted Lucille
through the raging
torrent known as Five
Finger Rapids. . . . We
let two large trees float
ahead of us and clear
the rapids. Watching
them run the rough course
made my palms sweat.

A huge sense of relief
swept over me once we
passed the big waves.
Five Finger Rapids has
been on my mind for
over a year. It was my
personal crux for the
entire trip. It is here
that we faced great
danger of someone going
in the water. An
enormous weight has
been lifted from me now.

—Matt

approach the rapids, and I'm not sure if I want to go through with it. But there is no turning back as the powerful water draws us in.

"Just keep it steady and straight," Matt hollers as he fights to control the boat.

One after one, the waves crest over the side of our canoe. A sudden jolt of cold shocks my body as water soaks my feet. I look down to see an inch of water in our boat. *Lucille* jerks back and forth as we bash through the series of rapids.

"Keep paddling!" Matt yells. I say nothing and focus on the calm water ahead. Somehow Matt has managed to keep *Lucille*'s bow straight, and we bounce a few more times before coming to a comfortable waver. Finally the water calms, and so do my nerves. I place the paddle in my lap and rest my shoulders. One big challenge down, hundreds more to go.

"That was awesome," Matt says excitedly.

"Yeah," I murmur, just glad I didn't die so early in the trip.

Situated on a steep bluff just downriver of the confluence of the Yukon and Pelly Rivers, the village of Fort Selkirk is spectacular. As part of an effort to landmark the historic settlement, many of the buildings have been repainted with bright colors and nearly every structure has been rebuilt to mimic its original façade. Wildflowers are in full bloom and complement the fields of fresh green grass. The view from the village is gorgeous. Distinctive basalt rock cliffs face the homes, and the impressive Victoria Rock rises just below the old town site.

We are welcomed to the campground by caretaker Maria Van Bibber. Wearing a straw hat with a fake sunflower attached to the front, the elderly woman walks the premises with confident ease. There are already several river travelers and restoration workers staying at Fort Selkirk. We see Margaret and Manfred in the distance. Van Bibber shows us a freshwater well, the outhouses, and several vacant campsites. As she walks us around, she explains that she was born and raised here and returns each summer to share Fort Selkirk's history with tourists.

Archaeological evidence shows that this site was occupied as far back as 7,000 years ago. The indigenous people are the Northern Tutchone, now known as the Selkirk First Nation. They relied on fishing and hunting for survival, and enjoyed a long history of trade with other First Nation tribes.

In the mid-1800s, when Hudson's Bay trader and explorer Robert Campbell established a trading post at Fort Selkirk, many of the Northern Tutchone and other

Fort Selkirk resident Maria Van Bibber talks to visitors at the preserved trading post near the junction of the Yukon and Pelly Rivers. Van Bibber was born in Fort Selkirk in 1923 and recently returned as summer caretaker.

tribes' traditional trade goods were in high demand. Traders sought furs, mother of pearl, cedar bark baskets, and special foods such as dried seal fat and seaweed. The post flourished until 1852, when the Chilkat Indians raided it to protect their trade monopoly. The story goes that the Chilkats tied Campbell to a raft and released it to float downstream. He was rescued, but kept moving east until he reached Montreal. Decades passed before another white man returned to the area. In 1889, an American named Arthur Harper successfully established a new post with his Native wife, Jennie Alexander, and operated throughout the Klondike gold rush. The Hudson's Bay Company returned in 1938 for a short time. But with the construction of the Klondike Highway and the decline in stern-wheeler activity, more local people moved away, and by the 1950s, Selkirk was abandoned. Today, the cement foundation is all that remains of the trading post. As we tour the site with Van Bibber, she explains how this was once a town of great excitement, symbolizing the future of an area that might someday be the capital of the Yukon Territory. Fort Selkirk is one of only a few early settlements on the Yukon River still largely intact, but a capital city never materialized.

As we settle in, paddlers stop by and visit, including Manfred and Margaret, who have big news: they plan to be married in Fort Selkirk the next day.

"Can you believe it?" Matt asks. "A wedding in Fort Selkirk? It's going to be beautiful!" I look around and think about what a wedding here would be like. Matt is already preparing his camera gear. He has always been the romantic, and I've been the realist. He sees the beauty of every moment before it even happens. I, on the other hand, can't imagine not being able to take a shower the day of my wedding.

"Don't get any ideas," I smile as he chooses which film to use.

"Who, me?" he says sarcastically.

The wedding takes place at St. Andrews Anglican Church, a gorgeous log structure built in 1931. It is one of three buildings remaining of the Anglican Church Mission at the old trading post. The building is the most elaborate structure in Fort Selkirk, with polished pews, hardwood floors, and stained glass windows. Once a

During their 2,000-mile canoe trip down the Yukon, Manfred Kuchenmuller and Margaret Moreau stop to exchange wedding vows in Fort Selkirk's historical St. Andrews Church. The couple pulled a tuxedo and wedding gown from their dry-bags, married, then continued paddling toward the Bering Sea for their honeymoon.

focal point of the community, St. Andrews has been used for services only occasionally since 1953.

There is no doubt that today the church is the focus of everyone's attention. A boat full of people arrives in the morning to witness the ceremony, including the magistrate from Pelly Crossing who will perform the ceremony. Matt and I watch as Manfred shaves at a picnic table and Margaret lays out her dress. Somewhere among their very simple supplies, they have packed a tuxedo jacket and a silk wedding gown. I look at the couple and notice Margaret does not have a bouquet. I quietly walk back into the woods and pick several fresh wildflowers. I then tear a piece off my bandana and tie the bouquet. The smell of fresh lupine and daisies fills the air.

When Margaret sees the bouquet she is thrilled. Matt looks at me as if I've accomplished a true wilderness miracle.

"What? Every bride needs a beautiful bouquet," I say. The magic of the Yukon takes over on the walk to the church. Everyone at camp shows up. It was the simplest wedding I have ever been to, but by far the most beautiful. It may as well be 1901.

It's JUNE 21—summer solstice—when we pull out of Fort Selkirk bound for Dawson City. We have been traveling for thirteen days and have covered just over 240 miles; Dawson lies 170 miles downriver. We dive back into the wilderness that spans these remote communities. For the next three days, it is just us, our thoughts, and *Lucille*. Paddling the Yukon is taking longer than we'd expected. After several hours in the canoe, we start to squirm restlessly in our seats and need to stretch our legs. Besides, there is so much to stop and explore along the way. Then there is the weather. Lately, gusting winds have often put a halt to our progress, quickly stirring the river into a torrent of three-foot waves. The only thing we can do is pull off and wait it out.

Today a storm came on so quickly we barely got off the river in time. Matt and I paddled over to an island bristling with sweepers—trees that have collapsed into the river from eroded banks and stick out into the current. The submerged logs threatened to turn over our canoe, and we almost become a Yukon statistic. The advice you always hear is: *Whatever happens, don't panic.* But we don't adhere to that. By the time we finally pull ourselves up through the brush and into a bug-infested forest,

June 22

Solstice came and went . . . so did my hopes to travel 50 miles today. Strong headwinds and heavy rains found us just 10 miles farther on the map. We make camp at a high bluff with two Germans. Both work as members of a German Swat team. They speak great English and offer us a hot drink as soon as we pull up. We are only 100 miles from Dawson, yet it seems like 1,000 miles away.

— Megan

June 23

Matt has forgotten to close the tent door and we are filled with bugs. Ugh. So much for a good night's rest.

— Megan

Megan takes time to journal at camp between the Big Salmon and Little Salmon Rivers.

we are exhausted and wet. Matt tries to construct a shelter with our blue tarp, but fails miserably. The wind and rain are blowing so hard that the tarp tangles into a big mess. He only succeeds in wrapping himself in the wet, blue nylon. I look on with a tuna sandwich and laugh.

"I'm not amused," he says.

"Just sit down and have a sandwich," I answer.

We sit on a log, wrapped in the blue tarp, waiting for the storm to pass.

The White River carves through the Wrangell–Saint Elias Mountains and crashes into the Yukon. The junction is enormous, and the river opens up with a horizon of nothing but dark gray rapids. It sounds as if we're dragging our canoe over a pile of gravel as we're sucked far out into the maze of silty channels. The pace of the water quickens and the canoe begins to buck up and down. We paddle nervously toward a point of land in the distance. I have that feeling again, the one that makes you sick to your stomach with fear. The landscape is so large. Miles of water and mountains dwarf *Lucille*. Matt says something, but I'm not listening. I am focusing on a small plot of land far in the distance. I paddle hard, feeling each pass through the swift water. *Lucille* cuts through the water fast, following our lead. Before I even realize it, we are just feet from the shore of an island. Another day, another unexpected challenge.

We coast into Klondike country on a sunny day. I actually lie back in the canoe and take a midmorning nap as we make the final bends into Dawson City. I feel better today, much better. A shower is now just a few hours away.

NAMED FOR GEORGE DAWSON, the director of the Canadian Geological Survey, Dawson City sits just above the spot where the Klondike River pours into the Yukon. On August 16, 1896, George Washington Carmack, Skookum Jim, and Tagish Charley discovered gold on Rabbit Creek, later renamed Bonanza Creek, in the hills south of here, spurring one of the greatest gold rushes in history. Dawson quickly became a tent city as word spread to mining camps up and down the Yukon River. By the following year, the population had grown to 5,000. At the height of the stampede to the Klondike goldfields, Dawson City was home to about 30,000. Chaos ensued as food stores, sanitation, and housing struggled to keep up. Supply ships failed to arrive before freeze-up that year, and many were left to starve. More than 2,000 men died of scurvy. Typhoid reached epidemic proportions and killed thousands. The entire town was razed by fire on several occasions. Nevertheless, the Yukon became a separate territory and Dawson its capital in 1898. As the thousands who traveled to the Klondike realized that all the claims had been staked a year before they arrived, the famous northern capital began to settle. Many returned home. Others moved on to different parts of Canada and Alaska in search of a wilderness life. When word arrived that people were panning gold from the beaches of Nome, Alaska, Dawson nearly emptied. Today Dawson City is a monument to this great movement of mankind.

DAWSON ARRIVES with as much fanfare as I expect. The campground is packed with people. Picnic tables and an outhouse make me smile. A shower is becoming less of a priority and an indoor bathroom more so. Swatting mosquitoes while trying to pee

June 23, Saturday
Ogilvie Island, Yukon
Territory

The wind has been our enemy. It bites at our faces as we try to make our way to Dawson City. For the past three days it has delayed us. We got trapped in a blowing thunderstorm on Thursday. Retreated to brushy island to change into our rain gear. Everything stopped after an hour and we got going again. . . . Later, we struggled for two more hours before pulling up on a muddy island. No other choice but to camp here on this bug-infested sandbar. And the line of bear tracks was a big hit with my partner.

—Matt

in the woods is getting old and scratching my rear end no longer seems appropriate in a city. I quickly set up the tent, no longer needing any help. A few minutes later, we hop on a large orange ferry that takes us across the river to Dawson City. It feels a little strange to be on the river and not in *Lucille*. The ride takes about five minutes, not fifty.

From the dirt roads to the gold-rush–era buildings, Dawson City is a historical treasure that looks like it has not changed for a century. We find a pizza joint with a patio and order a large pizza and two beers. We forget all about a hot shower.

In Dawson we are lucky to meet John Gould, a longtime Dawson gold miner. He recently wrote a book about his experiences. Generations of gold-mining families still live in Dawson, and the Goulds are one of them. John explains how his father staked fourteen claims in 1902. Matt and I ask him how we can get out to the goldfields.

"It's a long walk, but you can do it," Gould says unconvincingly. "Or, I can take you there if you need me to. Meet me here tomorrow afternoon." A day later, in 80-degree heat, we pile into Gould's vintage pickup truck. He tells us we're going to John Alton's gold mine. Once there, we see huge tractors move tons of dirt and rock. A conveyer belt separates the dust from rocks. Piles are resifted again and again to extract as much gold as possible. A small separator shows bright red, orange, and gold particles. The pieces will be filtered through water to extract the gold. Sitting in a small, black plastic gold pan is about a tablespoon of gold.

"One day's work," John Alton tells me, as he rubs his fingers through the dust. It is not worth much at all, but I get the feeling these men wouldn't trade their lives here for anything in the world.

On our last day in Dawson, we decide to visit the city's resident caveman, 38-year-old Bill Donaldson. His "patio" is filled with honey buckets, chicken droppings, and clothes that never made it to the laundry or trash, I can't figure out which. His cave is roughly 35 feet deep and barely five and a half feet tall. He lives there year-round. An old woodstove heats the place in the winter. A large piece of plywood covers the opening of the cave to keep the heat in and the bugs out. I can't imagine a worse fate, and I look at Matt in disgust.

Bill seems even more amused by his lifestyle than Matt and I. There is not much to show for 38 years of living. His bed is the backseat of a van. Old rusted coffee cans

▲ *Tipping back a "Sour Toe Cocktail" is a Yukon tradition. Stored in a case lined with rock salt, an amputated toe floats in the liquor of your choice. The toe must bump your lip for the drink to go on the record. Those who swallow the toe must replace the digit with one of their own.*

◄ *We caught this shopkeeper on her rush to work in Dawson City. Once the capital of the Yukon Territory, today's Dawson is a walk through a beautifully restored gold rush town.*

28312
DRIVERS
MUST REMAIN IN VEHICLE
DURING FERRY CROSSING
VEHICLE ENGINE TO BE
SHUT OFF
AND EMERGENCY BRAKE
TO BE APPLIED
PASSENGERS MUST KEEP
CLEAR OF RAMPS AND
SIDES AT ALL TIMES

Named for a past commissioner of the Yukon Territory, the George Black *ferries travelers across the Yukon River at Dawson City.*

June 24

Some days I doubt my ability to complete a trip like this, most days in fact. But with Matt it all seems possible. He paddles meticulously all afternoon while I rest. This is the man I love for sure. He sits by the fire and reads Robert Service poetry to me. This is his home. How will I fit in?

— Megan

hold silverware and some pens. A few pots hang from the stove. "Simpler is better," he says with a laugh. From the river it's difficult to see where Bill lives. Even today, if anyone ever told me a caveman lives along the banks of the Yukon I probably wouldn't believe them.

Two days later we arrive in the United States. A boundary line swath of clear-cut forest on both sides of the Yukon indicates where Canada ends and the United States begins. First established in 1887 by the famed Yukon surveyor William Ogilvie, the border was tested in the early days of the Klondike rush. A U.S. post office stood in the mining town of Fortymile in 1889, and Leroy Napoleon "Jack" McQuesten acted as postmaster. The community was regarded for many years as an Alaskan gold prospect even though it lay well within the Canadian boundary. The Royal Canadian Mounted Police arrived in 1895 to firm their claim on the lawless mining camp. Today flags from both countries hang from a line strung between two trees. There is no change in the landscape, but as we cross into Alaska, for some reason I feel a sense of relief and familiarity. We hop out of *Lucille* and climb up some boulders to the clearing. Back in the brush, a marble monument officially marks the border.

Bill "Caveman" Donaldson lives in a cave on the Yukon's western bank. Miners in the early 19th century excavated 35 feet of a mine shaft before giving up. Donaldson took up residence in 1996. "My dad loves it," he said, "because he can tell people that his son is 38 and still lives in a cave."

There is no outpost, border agent, or even a fence. Feeling very patriotic, we take several pictures, hop back into *Lucille*, and float into Alaska.

Our first stop in Alaska is the little town of Eagle, twelve miles west of the Alaska–Canada border on the Taylor Highway. Founded in 1897, it was the first incorporated city in the state's interior. Today it is a Historic District and National Landmark with many restored buildings, including Judge James Wickersham's lodge. In 1900, the Second and Third Judicial Districts were created for the northern portion of Alaska, still a lawless territory at the time. President McKinley appointed Wickersham as first judge for the Third Judicial District, headquartered at Eagle City. At the time, all crimes and conflicts were resolved by what was known as a miners' meeting. The accused was brought before his peers, who decided guilt and sentence, and executed punishment. It was a rough form of justice, and a man could easily be condemned to hang for a seemingly minor offense such as theft. To steal food stores from another miner in the far north was just as bad as murdering someone. Wickersham's court brought a more civilized form of due process to these fringes of society. His courthouse is still visible from the river.

We arrive just in time for the Fourth of July. Part of the celebration is a rifle shoot competition. From the moment we arrive, we hear the continual sound of men and women shooting rifles at targets about a quarter of a mile away across the river. One man shows up in a maroon leisure suit and pulls out a .44 magnum. He doesn't wait for the judges or anyone; he just begins to shoot his pistol off. When he's done, he places the pistol back in his pants pocket.

"This is a little weird, isn't it?" I ask Matt.

"This is Eagle, Alaska, Meg."

It is the epitome of freedom and liberty, and on the Fourth of July, Eagle now seems the most appropriate place to be. On the ground, men and women lie down and grab everything from a .22 to 30.06 and shoot at three bright orange targets on a beach across the river. Once in a while everyone screams, "Boat, boat, boat! Hold your fire!"

I turn around to tell Matt how crazy this is, but he's gone. Seconds later a man points to Matt lying on the ground, shooting a borrowed rifle. He misses the target every time, but he's sent me into a frenzy of laughter.

"Can't take the Alaska out of the man, huh?" I chide him when he returns.

July 2

USA here we come! We have now officially been living in a tent for over a month. I'm still okay with it. After a long day of travel, it's surprising how comforting a tent is. Today was a nice day— 10 hours, 52 miles to Fortymile River. You can go as far as you can push yourself.

— Megan

Three ounces is not a bad morning's work at John Alton's gold mine on Last Chance Creek outside of Dawson City. Alton tells us, "We'll be out of debt on Saturday." The small placer operation employs five other miners who work 15-hour days during the summer.

"Welcome home," Matt says.

The trip from Eagle to the small town of Circle is supposed to be gorgeous, but the beauty is hidden under thick clouds and heavy rain. The temperatures feel more like mid-March than early July as we paddle through the continuous downpour. The next 115 miles of the Yukon River are part of the Yukon–Charley Rivers National Preserve, 2.5 million acres of protected state and federal land. Access to land in the Yukon–Charley is a hotly contested issue in Alaska, as the region around Eagle was very popular with squatters who have since been evicted by the National Park Service. Weary prospectors who decided to make a go at trapping also settled the banks of the Yukon and its tributaries, such as the Charley River. These days the National Park Service maintains their cabins, and if you can find them along the river, you can use them.

After eight hours of paddling through the wind-driven rain, the Yukon merges with the Nation River, a small clear-water tributary. Matt finds the old Nelson cabin, the one we'd heard about from the park service, hidden in the dense spruce forest. Quickly we ferry our gear into the small log hut and get the fire to a dull roar in

Gold miner Jimmy Simpson shows off a 4-ounce nugget he found on the streets of Dawson City. Simpson and his wife, Marcene, moved to the Yukon to mine four claims on Irish Gulch and six on Moose Creek. "If the price of gold goes up to $300 (an ounce), we'll start mining again," he says.

Tom Christiano and his Yorkshire terrier, Chelsea, have been traveling in his "American Eagle" since he retired from the U.S. Coast Guard eight years ago. "We're doing what we want to do," he tells us. Christiano has visited every state except Rhode Island.

Gold mining and Bush living lured Al Wiggins to Eagle, Alaska, from Georgia in 1980. He helps mine a claim on American Creek.

the woodstove. In the 1930s, this was the home of Christopher Nelson, an old prospector and trapper who had a knack for almost nonstop talking when he entertained visitors. Soon the cabin feels as hot as a sauna and fills with steam from our drying rain gear. Outside the rain intensifies on the tin roof as we sip hot tea and play cards on the single bunk.

On our last night in the preserve, we throw our sleeping bags down on the hardwood floor of Slaven's Roadhouse, a two-story log bunkhouse with a huge woodstove, 50 miles downriver from Nelson's cabin. The National Park Service now runs the roadhouse that was built by Frank Slaven in 1917. He arrived during the 1898 stampede to the Klondike and eventually moved down the Yukon. Today there are other cabins nearby for visitors and a gravel road leading to the Coal Creek gold dredge. The dredge is a short walk back into the woods. After getting settled, Matt and I make the journey. It is one of our last big gold-rush sites on the Yukon. The dredge, built in 1935, is enormous and sits stranded in rusty water. We walk around inside and stick our heads into the dark, menacing machinery used to separate the gold from the gravel. Except for the birds maneuvering in and out of the ceiling beams, the dredge is empty.

Circle, Alaska, once boasted the distinction of being the largest log cabin town in the world. Established in 1894 as a result of a gold strike on neighboring Birch Creek, it was also known as the "Paris of the North" due to its relative level of sophistication. The community hosted the only opera house on the Yukon River, as well as a library, two theaters, and eight dance halls. The population swelled to about 3,000 at one time, but the town quickly grew deserted when word of the Klondike drifted downriver.

The Steese Highway, a rough washboard gravel road, comes to an abrupt end at Circle, connecting the river to Fairbanks. We could hitch the 162 miles and be home in a matter of hours. I'm ashamed to admit that I feel slightly tempted to stick out my thumb. I look at Matt, busy preparing dinner at our riverside camp. The twinkle in his eye remains bright, a reflection of the sudden change in the weather. After a week of steady rain and wind, the sun finally broke through the clouds late in the day. Tonight there is a vibrant double rainbow arched over the Yukon. If someone or something is trying to talk to me, it's working. Strangely I no longer feel like getting near the road.

July 2

Ended our 10-hour day at the mouth of the Fortymile River. Tall grass hosts voracious mosquitoes. Lucky for us there is a small cabin to use. Threw our sleeping bags right on the bed; first time sleeping off the ground in nearly a month.

—Matt

Flat-bottom powerboats line the bank of the Yukon in the village of Circle, Alaska. During the summer fishing season, riverboats are at work around the clock checking fish wheels and nets.

PART II

YOOKKENE

Circle to Koyukuk, Alaska

At Fort Yukon, the river is said to be seven miles wide.... At this point, one thousand miles from the river's mouth and about the same distance from its head, the river sweeps with a marked curve into the arctic regions, and then, with less enthusiasm than most polar seekers, turns back into the temperate zone, having been in the arctic for less than a league, and, as the current runs, for less than an hour. The early traders at Fort Yukon supposed their river ran parallel to the Mackenzie; and so it was mapped, its bed being continued north to where its hypothetical waters were poured into the Arctic Sea. The conservative slowness of the English to undo what the English have done had a new illustration as late as 1883, when one of the best of English globe-makers, in a work of art in his line, sent the Yukon with its mighty but unnamed tributaries still into the Arctic. There it will be made to flow until some Englishman shows that it surely flows elsewhere.

— Lt. Frederick Schwatka, 1883

The shouting cuts across the water and breaks the silence of the mile-wide river. Adrift on the currents, we spot the tiny figure of a man hailing us from the far bank. Arms waving, he asks us to join him for lunch. We had just pushed off from Circle the day before, after tending to a list of chores in the small Athabascan village: laundry, filling water

Megan takes a break on a small island in the vast Yukon Flats National Wildlife Refuge.
The Yukon River spreads into a 10-mile-wide braided maze through the refuge.

Athabascan Chief Isaac Johnson and two others traverse the river in traditional birch-bark canoes.
[PHOTO BY CHARLES F. METCALF: ALASKA STATE LIBRARY, ALASKA PURCHASE CENTENNIAL COMMISSION COLLECTION, PCA #20-51]

bags, phone calls, and arranging for our next box of groceries to be shipped out from Fairbanks. This stranger's invitation to share a meal echoes repeatedly down the river, making it even more appealing. We quickly change course. During July on the middle Yukon, meals usually mean king salmon. We answer his offer with rapid paddle strokes.

We have floated into the heart of Athabascan country, which reaches from behind us, in Canada's Yukon Territory, to well beyond us—extending to just a few hundred miles shy of the Bering Sea. The Koyukon people who lived in this region called the waterway *Yookkene* for "big river." For centuries the Native peoples have depended on the salmon runs provided by the river.

Adlai Alexander coaches us into a side slough where we dock next to his flat-bottomed powerboat. He takes our bowline in the no-nonsense manner brought about by a life on the river, and helps me onto the muddy shore. A huge man with a Yukon-sized smile, he welcomes us to his summer fish camp and leads the way into the dense stand of black spruce, his ponytail falling to the back of a dirty flannel shirt.

A collection of ragged blue tarps pulled tight on spruce-pole frames mix with several canvas wall tents in Alexander's one-man camp. His son Jeremiah and nephew Cody Agli play one-on-one in a dusty clearing with a basketball hoop nailed to a tree. The older Jeremiah slips past his smaller cousin for a lay-up. Alexander brings the boys down from the village of Fort Yukon for a week at a time. "It keeps them out of trouble and from driving their grandmother crazy," he says.

The acrid smell of alder smoke mixes with a strong salmon scent. Alexander's smoke shack is a collection of aluminum siding, blue plastic, and old lumber. Thick smoke pours from every hole in the tall shed. A crude table crafted from scrap plywood stands bloodstained under a covering of tarps. Large knives lie where they were put down after the last catch. Out on the water a stiff wind picks up as we sit and trade stories under a billowing blue tarp. The conversation drifts from one topic to the next, slow and steady like the river. Our host quickly hands out cups of black tea while the entrée of salmon and potatoes simmers on his Coleman stove. Lunch is served buffet style, with our contributions of potato chips and trail mix. All you can eat. I shovel in another mouthful of the bright orange fish, cooked to perfection.

Adlai gives us the grand tour, showing us where we can pitch our tent for the night. As I look out over the river I notice that high winds have worked the Yukon into a fury of whitecaps, and thunder booms in the distance. We had wanted to travel 30 miles farther today, but after seeing the turbulent water, there's no doubt we're staying.

Matt and I take turns reading in a comfortable hammock overlooking the river. Later I get a lesson in splitting wood with an ax, much to Matt's amusement. Dinner is served on an old couch sitting outside next to a hot woodstove. We start to settle into river time. Adlai asks us if we wouldn't mind keeping an eye on his camp that night while he brings his son and nephew back to town. Matt and I agree and thank him for his hospitality as he loads up his boat with smoked salmon. We exchange smiles and wave good-bye.

The next morning we paddle toward the Yukon Flats National Wildlife Refuge, a nine-million acre wetland expanse bisected by the Yukon River. It is the third-largest conservation area in the National Wildlife Refuge System. We had heard all sorts of warnings about this part of the river, from steering clear of the braided channels, to getting eaten alive by mosquitoes. So far we are having great luck. The previous week's rain has created a nice current moving us along quickly.

July 8

We arrived in Circle last night. We needed to get some work done here. I took a hot shower and washed some clothes. By 1 we were back on the river. Because of last week's rain, the river is high and fast. We are thankful for no rain for the first time in over a week.

—Megan

Long sandbars with little vegetation provide great campsites free of bugs. Our choice tonight even has a freshwater pool. Actually it's a depression in the sand that has filled with rainwater, but it's still a luxury on the muddy Yukon. I feel like a new woman after taking a short sponge bath. Matt and I have to catch up on some journal writing tonight. We cozy up to a log in the warm evening sun, the calm river passing as we write about the last few days. Some bluegrass music plays on the portable compact disc player as we watch two mergansers cut effortlessly upriver. I glance at Matt, his sunburned face casting a shadow on his notebook. He looks up at me, smiles, and without saying a word let's me know that he is relishing this moment as much as I am. I imagine we are the only two people ever to have sat in this gorgeous spot, and we are captivated by the moment.

There is something about the "flats." The actual landscape of the area may be flat, but it is no less beautiful. Dark-green spruce forests cut the riverbank and billowing white clouds line the endless sky. It is this kind of raw wilderness that attracts people from all over the world, including a trio of paddlers from Switzerland.

We first met Roland Thur, Simon Uhlmann, and Rene Zach in Dawson City, where they left a note of introduction on our tent. Like us, they too are planning to paddle the entire Yukon. It's reassuring to know there are other "floaters" keeping an eye out for us. When we arrive in Fort Yukon, the trio meets us with a case of beer and invites us to camp on an island across from the village. The Swiss offer us some great perspective on our trip. For them coming to Alaska is a dream. Switzerland is a magnificent country, but they have come all this way for an adventure they tell us they can't get anywhere in Europe. They cook over enormous campfires every night and carve their cooking tools from driftwood. For three months they plan to drink straight from the river. They learn how to play the harmonica and compose ballads about the Yukon. That night the orange glow of the fire, and the blue and purple sunset at midnight, illuminate the faces of five people from two different continents. Though we do not speak the same language, we are each experiencing what so many people come here for—the simple rugged beauty of interior Alaska. It is like no other place in the world. The subtle beauty grabs your attention when you least expect it: from warm summer sunsets that fill your soul, to January hoarfrost glinting as it clings to birch. As I fall asleep, I can't help but smile. In a few weeks these men from Switzerland will have to go home, but I get to live here.

Salmon fillets are hung to dry at the Solomon family fish camp near the village of Fort Yukon, Alaska. Relatives from around the state try to spend at least a week at the traditional camp on the river, subsistence fishing, relaxing, and catching up.

Swiss travelers Rene Zach, Simon Uhlmann, and Roland Thur make camp in the Yukon Flats National Wildlife Refuge on their journey from Whitehorse to the Bering Sea. "We came for the wilderness, to camp on the islands, and to build big fires," says Thur.

Established by the British Hudson's Bay Company as a trading post at the confluence of the Porcupine and Yukon Rivers, Fort Yukon stood as the center of commerce in Alaska's interior in the mid-1800s. Grizzled trappers would haul their stacks of furs into town and ship them to outside markets. Dirty prospectors purchased their yearly outfits here. And the Gwich'in people, weary of their endless pursuit of the caribou herds, settled at this spot. Even though some of the Alaska Natives live in wood-sided homes much like the ones you might see in Fairbanks or Anchorage, to this day, they still rely on this great land to fill their souls as well as their stomachs.

We first meet the Solomon family on a long sandbar just outside of Fort Yukon. As we paddle *Lucille* up to shore, I smile as the children chase each other in and out of the water, enjoying the simple pleasures of summer on the river. Robert Solomon is keeping an eye on his nieces and nephews while mending a long gill net spread across the sand. A dirty ball cap keeps his thick, black hair out of his face while weathered hands move quickly through the net, tying off any holes. "It's not easy," Robert says about subsistence fishing. "It's a lot of work and it costs a lot of money." But fishing Yukon salmon is a tradition his family depends on. He points to a swath of blue tarps in the tree line across from the island, revealing his family's summer camp. "Come have some lunch," he says.

A stretch of swift water separates us from the Solomon fish camp on the opposite bank. We look at each other doubtfully; it will require hard paddling to ferry across the river.

We slide *Lucille* back into the river and begin deep paddle strokes. As we are learning, you don't turn down an invitation on the Yukon River. Socializing is an important part of living out here, and fish camp is no exception.

As with so many Fort Yukon elders, the lines creasing Hannah Solomon's face tell their own story. Hers speak of a loving family and hard wilderness living. In her 90s, she takes great pride in her camp, and surveys her Yukon estate. The matriarch of the family, Hannah swats flies off the plywood table, making sure everyone has more than enough to eat. She points to her smokehouse and hundreds of bright orange salmon hanging underneath blue tarps nailed to spruce boughs. Smoke pours from small slits in the tarp as salmon strips inhale the burning of fresh alder. "Before, five years ago, we got lots of fish, fill up the whole cache," she says, swatting a mosquito. "Now we got 26 the other day." Hannah says this year's run has not been as good as in the past. For her, one summer at fish camp feeds a community all winter long. "We share with everyone—family, friends, potlatch."

Village elder Daniel Flint enjoys a sunny afternoon outside his home in Fort Yukon. Most villages along the river subscribe to satellite television.

Recent summers have brought subsistence closures, and families like the Solomons have been forced to do more with less. During the salmon runs, the Alaska Department of Fish and Game and the Federal Subsistence Board dictate a schedule for fishermen, dependent on the number of salmon heading up into the Yukon drainage. Openings can range from several days to a few hours per week, and they change frequently during the season. Current regulations and updates are broadcast in the evening, with Yukon families gathered around battery-powered radios—if they have them. We camp on a rocky beach and talk about fish camp over dinner. It's hard to believe that in a place so far into the wilderness there could be such strict, confusing rules for fishing.

The hundreds of channels that make up the Yukon Flats intersect each other and we float unknowingly from one to the next. I'm confused, if not completely lost, in the endless maze of waterways. Farther upriver, mountains and distinct bluffs offered us reference points to gauge our location. Today, the slough we have been traveling on is getting narrower and narrower. We have heard horror stories from other Yukoners about paddling into a dead end and fighting the current back the way you came. By mid-afternoon I wonder if maybe we're lost. Matt tries to pinpoint our location on a topographic map where one inch spans about five miles. Our summer voyage will take us across 20 such maps, on which villages are tiny dots and the immense Yukon a thin blue line.

"We are coming up on this here," he says, pointing confidently to the tip of an island. Skeptical of his accuracy, I roll my eyes.

"There is no way you can tell that from this map," I say.

"Look, this is the back of an island, not the other side of the river," Matt says, trying to convince me. Ten minutes later the slough opens to the Yukon's main channel, proving to be the backside of the island Matt had just pointed to.

"Oops," I say, smiling. I was wrong, but I'm relieved to find that he knows where we are.

The 90-degree heat is getting to us, although we know from experience that the Interior is a region of extremes. The village of Fort Yukon, just above the Arctic Circle, set the state's record high temperature of 100 degrees in 1915. Amazing when you consider that winter temperatures can hover at 50 degrees—below zero— for weeks.

I look up and notice thousands of puffy white clouds, but for some reason there is no shade out in the flats. We think we see a bear, but it's a rock. We think we see a moose, but it's a tree. Suddenly I hear Matt shout, "How's it going?" I look over to see whom he is waving at, but nobody is there.

"Who are you shouting to?" I ask. Matt looks closer and then quickly stops waving. "Oh," he says embarrassed, "I thought that was a person," he says, pointing to an old rusted barrel lying on the bank. I laugh and offer him some water, telling him to drink the whole bottle and put a hat on. The hot sun makes some days longer than they should be.

I put my hand up to block the sun's rays and am finally able to see the village of Beaver. A large red building is flanked by several smaller buildings that make up the town. A steep rocky embankment leads to a bluff overlooking the river. We meet Cliff Adams almost immediately. Badly in need of a haircut, Matt had been following the sound of Cliff's shears from down the road. We find Cliff in the middle of getting a trim on his front porch. Short and stout with a round face split by a constant smile, he is friendly and approachable. After a short introduction, he

July 15

This is the most spectacular day of the trip so far. There is not a cloud in the sky and the sun is just beaming down on us. We are thrilled. It's a little hot for Matt, but we keep busy most of the day reading and writing. By 7 p.m. we are in Beaver and set up camp.

— Megan

Arluk Smoke was born in Beaver, Alaska, and has no reason to leave. Speaking of his ancestors, he tells us, "Here, I walk with the Great Ones."

Jenny Pitka shares stories about growing up in Beaver. Beyond her, local fishermen are returning from checking their set nets downriver.

invites Matt onto the deck for a trim. Five minutes later, Matt's hair almost all gone, he invites us to check his nets with him that afternoon.

Cruising across the river in a motorboat is a strange sensation for me. In *Lucille* it will take us months to paddle the length of the river, but if we had a motorboat it might take us less than two weeks. The speed is a nice change. Several of Cliff's family members are along for the ride. They have two nets set up in two different eddies just across the river from Beaver. One after the next, his nephew pulls in bright red king salmon. The salmon flip uncontrollably in a metal bin, sending slime all over me. I try to act cool and wipe the slime from my face, but Cliff notices my discomfort. He smiles at me from behind the steering wheel. If I think I am fooling anyone I am wrong. Most people sense I am out of my element. Thankfully, almost everyone we've met treats me like I've lived here my whole life.

After docking in Beaver, Cliff grabs a knife and a salmon and gets to work. He cuts the fish precisely down the center; then, holding the fish by its tail, he runs the knife over the inside of the pink meat before handing it over to the drying rack. His family works from the village instead of traveling out to fish camp. Husbands and wives, sisters and brothers all gather in an assembly line. The work goes on for over an hour until the tables are clean and each knife is hung back on a wooden beam.

A collective sigh rises from the adults. Several little kids grab their life jackets and head for the river. A small skiff passes the kids, dousing them as they bob in a set of small waves. Their excited screams can be heard throughout the village. The driver smiles and turns around for another pass, sending more waves into the cheering youngsters. He finally pulls into shore and a plastic bin showcases his catch of kings. Soon, the fish-cleaning process will start all over again for another family.

Back at our camp that night several people stop by to talk. We smell the liquor on one woman before she even sits down. Although we try to talk to her about Beaver, she says very little and what she does say is difficult to understand. Without saying good-bye she slowly walks away. The hot sun is just cooling off, but I feel the intensity of my day. Some here are working to preserve what little they have left; others have already given up. This pull of opposites plagues rural Alaska. I feel sympathy for those who can't make it happen and pride for those who can. When I meet

Jake Thomas and his father, Jerry, show off their catch. The family has been learning how to subsistence fish since moving back to Beaver, the home of Jerry's wife, Carol Pitka-Thomas.

July 18

40 days! Yikes! Windy rough water until this afternoon, but we are now only 30 miles from Stevens.

— Megan

families working hard at fish camp, I want to fight alongside them to make sure their way of life is preserved, just like the summer's catch, sealed tightly in a jar, until someone comes along to open it up so they can smell and taste how good it really is.

A CLIMB UP a short, steep embankment reveals a disenchanting view of Stevens Village. One of the largest buildings is falling apart. As we walk the village's only dirt road, we can't help but notice that many of the homes lining the riverfront are boarded up. Our canoe sits in a dump of soda cans, old outboard motors, and broken canning jars. We do not want to camp here, but the post office is already closed and a box of groceries awaits us. The only place to set up camp is in a snowmobile graveyard on the riverfront. Tonight an old snowmachine seat serves as our tabletop.

The village store is a tiny log structure, and there are a few people milling around out front sucking on Popsicles. "There is a God!" I whisper to Matt. The temperature has once again reached the 90s. Before unpacking the boat we go to buy a frozen treat. The few supplies in the store fit easily into a space about six feet square. The room is dark and damp. The store owner sits in a lawn chair next to the cash register. About a dozen shelves offer an assortment of candy bars and other snacks. The food looks like it's been there for a while.

I lean up to Matt's ear and whisper, "I'm glad we are picking up supplies at the post office in the morning."

"Me, too," he whispers back, smiling.

A refrigerator lines a wall to our right. Inside Matt digs out two Popsicles as the store owner watches us closely. We walk back outside savoring the cool treat. When I turn around to go back to the boat, I'm caught off guard by the late-afternoon sun reflecting off the river. It's a lovely view. I turn around and look at Stevens and then back at the sun. This, I think, must be what the people of Stevens look at every day. They probably do not even notice the dilapidated buildings anymore.

The next morning we walk across town to the post office. Two large boxes sit under a shelf. They arrived general delivery weeks ago. Matt had placed a frozen block of cheese in one, hoping it might last. I tried to warn him against it; now, as he smells the cheese from the front door, he knows why.

It takes us about an hour to walk the 40-pound boxes back to our tent. We tear eagerly into them, pulling out all our new goodies: bags of chips, boxes of candy bars, new varieties of pasta. Sitting in the grass, sorting through our new supplies, is like getting a fresh start. All the labels are new, unlike the heavily weathered cans and boxes sitting in our waterproof food bag. To keep our load manageable, we promptly get rid of the older food items to make room for our favorites. The rearranging helps break up our three-month journey into smaller chunks: our next resupply point will be in Galena. It's another chore that adds time to our day, but neither of us seems to mind as we munch on some cheese puffs. The Dalton Highway Bridge is our next destination, and a mere 18 miles downriver. A late start shouldn't prevent us from getting there before evening.

Another afternoon storm catches us off guard and the wind quickly turns the water into three-foot swells. We no longer shout at each other in panic; we know what to do. Paddling as fast as we can, we make a mad dash for the shore. That's when I see a big black bear wandering back and forth, just waiting for us to land.

"Oh, good God," I yell as I begin paddling backwards.

Jason Burgess gets a haircut in the village of Stevens, Alaska.

July 21

Floated under the
Dalton Highway bridge
last night. This marks
the halfway point of our
journey. Weather has
been great; short stormy
periods followed by hot,
sunny afternoons. If this
keeps up, we'll make it to
the Bering Sea without
a hitch.

—Matt

"Check it out," Matt laughs happily—and reaches for his camera. Quickly, my eyes shoot back at him, and he sets his camera case down and grabs his paddle.

"Now what, Einstein?" I ask.

"Relax," he says, "It's not going to eat you."

I feel completely vulnerable. We have no choice but to get off the river, but a bear currently patrols the only stretch of open shoreline. Crossing the half-mile-wide river in the storm is not an option. I bang my paddle rapidly against the side of *Lucille*, yelling "Hey bear!" several times. When it doesn't work I scream louder. On shore, the bruin casually looks up and wanders back into the brush.

"What are you doing?" Matt asks, knowing he has just lost another great photo opportunity.

"I'm trying to decrease my chances of dying!" I reply with dire certainty. Matt rolls his eyes and keeps up the paddle stroke. We pull to the far end of the bank and examine the fresh tracks. By now the rain is pouring. Matt takes cover back in the brush with his camera, hoping for a picture, but I'm not taking any chances with the bear. I sink into the hood of my rain jacket, turn my back to the river, and stand next to *Lucille* scanning the bushes frantically. A half hour later the rain stops, and we push off again. I'm soaked, but happy to be alive.

WE'VE BEEN ON THE RIVER for nearly two months as we arrive at the Dalton Highway Bridge, the halfway point of our summerlong voyage. Here, the braided channels of the Yukon Flats come to an abrupt end and the entire river is brought together, flowing through a single gash on the horizon. Steep, forested hills rise directly from the shoreline as we leave behind the open floodplain. We're a couple of weeks behind schedule if we want to complete the journey in three months. Still, we've traveled about 1,000 miles of the Yukon River and we've been very lucky. Neither one of us has gotten sick, despite eating strange new foods at several fish camps. There have been no injuries so far, not even a pocketknife cut. I have already regained the 10 pounds I lost the first two weeks due to nerves. I am actually starting to put on weight. The only minor complaint we have is that after 12 hours a day on average of sitting in the canoe, our butts are a little sore.

The bridge, an enormous, man-made monstrosity catches us off guard. We lean back in our seats to watch the span pass over us as we float through its piers. It is the only bridge to cross the Yukon River in Alaska and it bears the last stretch of highway we'll see. According to the state of Alaska, the bridge is made out of 4,838 tons of structural steel, contains 170,000 bolts, and is 2,290 feet long. Its price tag: a mere $30 million. The bridge also supports the trans-Alaska oil pipeline. Every day about one million gallons of oil flow from Prudhoe Bay through 800 miles of pipe to Valdez.

With the discovery of oil on the Arctic slope in 1968, the idea was born for a pipeline to carry that crude to market. The three-year-long project began in early 1974 and culminated in the largest economic boom Alaska has ever seen. The $8-billion project reportedly employed over 70,000 people. Thousands of other jobs were connected to the project as well. In the 1970s, it seemed like half of Alaska was working on the pipeline. The span over the Yukon River was completed in 1975, and the first Prudhoe Bay oil reached the tidewater port in Valdez on August 1, 1977.

We camp a few feet below the bridge, and for the first time we marvel at something other than wildlife.

The E. L. Patton Bridge spans the Yukon River at the Dalton Highway in Alaska. Measuring 2,290 feet, the wooden-decked bridge marks the 1,000-mile mark of our journey from Lake Laberge. The trans-Alaska oil pipeline also crosses the Yukon at this point.

IT'S BEEN FOUR DAYS since we last had a shower. For Matt this is not a problem. Lately he's been stripping down and washing in the Yukon.

"Come on in, it's fine" he says splashing his chest with the silty brown liquid.

"You couldn't pay me enough!" I shout back, smiling. I do wash my hair in the river, but bathing is not an option. The water flows thick, like mud, and I'm convinced I wouldn't end up any cleaner. This morning I opt for a shower at the truck stop. I'm shocked to learn it will cost me $7. In the villages a few quarters at the washeteria do the trick. It's worth it though. Along the Yukon you never know when you'll get another hot shower.

Back in the canoe after leaving the Dalton Highway and just around the bend, a dark figure catches our eye. At first we thought it was a dog running loose on the banks of the Yukon. Along the river many people leave their dogs on islands and let them wander. But this dog looks too big.

"That's not a dog," Matt says. I squint my eyes to get a better look. We drift in as far as *Lucille* will go and watch the animal pace along the beach. It's a wolf, as black as onyx. At first it does not even notice us. As calmly and quietly as he can, Matt raises his camera. The wolf approaches 100 feet off our bow. It's gorgeous. I don't dare move. Then, in an instant, the sound of Matt's camera sends the animal running into the alders.

Watching wildlife has left us breathless throughout our journey. We have seen white-tailed deer, moose, bear, lynx, fox, and countless bald eagles. But my first encounter with a wolf—with its piercing eyes staring us down—is something I will never forget. Someone once told me that if you ever see a wolf in the wild consider yourself lucky. Now I know why.

The Yukon's single channel bends its way 60 miles to the village of Rampart. There is no danger of getting lost. The July sun beats down on us as we kick back for a lazy day in the canoe. We cycle through a routine of reading, paddling, and talking about whatever comes to mind. A short lunch break on a sandbar lets us stretch our legs. Farther downriver, a man waves to us from the front porch of his log cabin. We continue on.

After a long hot day in the canoe, I watch from our camp in Rampart as two boys repeatedly climb onto the top of their boat and, without a care in the world, jump 10 feet into the air before splashing in the Yukon's silty water. Again and again, to the delight of a group of adults standing on shore, they fly into the river. Their bodies silhouetted by the setting sun, each jump captures the innocence of a summer on the Yukon. From 100 yards away, I could see the smiles on their faces. That such a harsh land could offer such simple happiness should not have come as a surprise.

Several craggy cliffs at Rampart act as geographic landmarks, and we can easily trace our way downriver into the canyon. The Yukon squeezes its way between mountain peaks that lead down to cobbled shorelines and eroded embankments. A carpet of spruce and birch clings to the steeply rising slopes, hiding the occasional collection of blue tarps that marks a family's summer fish camp. An island composed of large boulders breaks up the river around the bend. The sound of the water rushing through the granite makes us a little bit nervous, and we grab tight to our paddles. Matt scopes the river and says we should stay left. Clearly labeled as "rapids" on our USGS maps, it is nothing compared to those we encountered at Five Fingers. Still, the current is forceful and one bad move could send us quickly into the rocks. After nearly two months in the canoe, our well-practiced skills pay off and we steer *Lucille* straight through the heart of the canyon.

A black wolf patrols the banks near the village of Rampart, Alaska. We went silent, letting our canoe drift onto the banks. The wolf slowly approached to just a hundred feet off our bow.

Rampart resident Paul Evans enjoys a swim in the Yukon River after helping his uncle check salmon nets all day.

David Bowen pulls in a net full of chinook salmon. Bowen catches as many as 20 fish in his three gill nets after leaving them overnight.

Almost as soon as we land on the beach, we know there is something different about Stan Zuray's summer residence. Maybe it's the hot tub fashioned out of an old fish crate, or the wall tent with the latest in computer technology, or the networks of pipes that provide running water. With his thick Boston accent he gives us the grand tour. Stan came to Alaska to live off the land, spending his first years in the country homesteading on the Tozitna River, north of Tanana. Now he does contract work with the U.S. Fish and Wildlife Service, assessing the summer salmon runs. His project is a combination of modern technology and subsistence living. Stan has created what he likes to call a "fish-friendly fish wheel." Each fish is caught, photographed, and then returned to the river within seconds. The images are sent back via microwave to Stan's research lab at his camp. Stan says that, in the past, agencies trying to assess the run would catch the fish and hold them in tanks before returning them to the river. Many fish, he says, got confused and died. With the runs declining, Stan wanted to help find a way to assess the run without making matters worse by harming the fish.

We sit and have tea with Stan and his neighbors, Charlie Campbell and Ruth Althoff. They share stories of the river, and I fall in love with the Yukon just listening to them. Life here is hard work, but there is also a joyful simplicity to it that appeals to me. At the end of the day, you sit down and talk with friends, instead of watching television. The pleasure of good company is a luxury on the river, for travelers and for residents. People tell you exactly what they think, not what they think you want to hear. There is no complaining, just facts-of-life information. I listen to the conversation, as Stan passes me more salmon strips and helps himself to our bag of cookies. His plywood cabin, lit by a lantern, is warm and cozy. My body craves the good food, good drink, and good company. There is no place else we would rather be.

Matt puts his arm around my shoulder as we listen to tales of the Yukon. I look at him and notice his dirty flannel shirt, long beard, and rosy cheeks. He joins in the conversation as if he has known our new friends his entire life. It makes sense to me

Sunset on the Yukon River at the village of Rampart. Residents use powerboats or aircraft to access the remote community.

Joseph and Katlyn Zuray soak in a fish crate hot tub at the family's fish camp on the Yukon River near Tanana. A double-barrel woodstove heats the river water before piping into the plastic tote.

how well Matt fits in with our company. He too is generous, easygoing, and always so refreshing.

The hospitality of the Yukon clearly follows us downriver. Stan invites us to stay in his guest room, a large tent already set up on the bank. We're thankful not to have to pitch camp for a couple of nights. Then, Charlie and Ruth tell us we can stay in their log home in Tanana, about 20-miles downriver from Stan's. We take them up on their invitation, as we wait out some bad weather.

The couple built the two-story cabin by hand a few years ago, harvesting and floating logs down the Tanana River. Rough-cut on the outside, for us it was like staying at a luxury hotel. After nearly two months, I finally get to sleep on a mattress.

The village itself is large. Located at the confluence of the Tanana and Yukon Rivers, Tanana is a central hub for many interior communities. The ancient Native trading site called *Nuchalawoya*, or "between the rivers," used to be located very close to Tanana. Koyukon Athabascans are the original inhabitants of the area, and hundreds still live a subsistence lifestyle here. There are no roads, and most people hunt, trap, and fish using interior trails and the river as their highways.

There are plenty of chores waiting for us in Tanana. Our first stop is the washeteria. We haven't done laundry since Beaver and our clothes stink. For the first time in my life I'm living in the same outfit day after day, a synthetic zip tee and a pair of khaki travel pants. Back in May when Matt first handed me the small dry-bag and said that it would be my suitcase, I almost fell over.

"I'll be lucky if I can get my socks and underwear in here," I screamed.

"Believe me Meg, the less stuff the better," he said.

It took me several days to plan out exactly what I wanted to take. Time and again I would rearrange the clothes, adding a favorite T-shirt, then painfully taking away that extra pair of wool socks. Everything had to fit in the equivalent of a small sleeping bag sack.

"You do not need two cotton T-shirts," Matt said one afternoon as I agonized over what to bring.

"Cotton is comfort," I whined.

"If you fall in the river in cotton, you'll die," Matt said harshly.

Now as I sit in the Tanana laundromat, I grab my long-sleeved black cotton T-shirt and hug it. I seldom wear it on the river, but when we get into town it is the first thing I change into. It is one luxury I'm glad I did not do without.

We are not in a rush to leave this busy little town. The weather is bad and we have a great place to stay. We peruse the Campbells' bookshelves, hungry for something new to read. Our trip has given me the opportunity to enjoy several books I've wanted to read for years. I spend hours every night reading in the tent. The only problem is—I didn't bring enough books along. In most village washeterias there is some sort of book exchange, usually a pile of well-worn paperbacks. All along the Yukon, Harlequin romance novels are very popular and there are plenty for the taking.

"These look awful," Matt adds. "What are you going to do?"

I smile and lay down the two books I brought to trade and grab two romance novels.

"How bad can they be?" I say. The thought of not having a book is worse than the thought of reading about some tacky romance.

For two days we eat lunch at the small café in the back of the grocery store. We even watch *Leaving Las Vegas* at Charlie and Ruth's. Completely shocked by the

Once a subsistence fisherman, Stan Zuray uses his knowledge of Yukon salmon for research projects with the U.S. Fish and Wildlife Service at his fish camp in the Rampart Canyon.

Salmon hang to cure in a smokehouse in the village of Rampart. Fillets are soaked in a brine and dry outside before moving into the smokehouse.

We join the Campbell family on a hike to the top of Bald Mountain, high above the Yukon River near Tanana. The Campbells live in the village, but spend summers at their cabin fish camp in the Rampart Canyon.

sensory overload, we both agreed later it was probably not a good idea. A story about drugs and alcohol in Las Vegas threatened to kill our river romance.

The weather is not getting any better, but we reluctantly decide to take off after breakfast. Canoeing through pouring rain, cold wind, and three-foot swells is not fun. After two hours we both admit we probably should have overstayed our welcome. "I'm done," I say wiping rainwater from my face. "Me, too," Matt shouts back. We look ahead toward a small island.

"I think that will work," Matt says, pointing to some trees. "Let's put the tent back in those bushes." The rain continues to pummel us. When we pull onto the beach, we notice that the camp spot is low to the water and might get flooded out. Still, exhausted and cold, we put up our tent and make some warm tea. About an hour later we step outside and notice the water is rising quickly. Now that we have passed the confluence of the Tanana River, the Yukon is taking on a lot more runoff.

"Quick, we need to move the tent!" Matt shouts.

"Are you kidding?" I ask.

"Move!" Matt yells with authority. I close my mouth and start pulling out tent stakes. The higher ground is not much higher and Matt questions our safety, but the river is too dangerous to travel on now.

"It's going to have to do," he says.

Neither of us sleeps well that night.

The weather is getting worse, not better. The Yukon is fast, high, and frothing. In certain spots, the water is a continuous series of wind-driven rapids that force us to shore in a panic. We spend an entire day bobbing in three-foot waves just off the bank in a desperate attempt to make a few miles. It is late July and already we can feel the season changing. In northern Alaska fall comes quickly and unexpectedly.

"Do you think we'll get any more nice days?" I ask pessimistically.

"Of course," Matt says, smiling. Even in the pouring rain, he's still so happy to be here. Every day the adventure gets better for him. Matt's attitude helps, and I force myself to forget about the weather and just enjoy camp. We crawl into our tent, and I devour my first cheesy romance novel. Life could definitely be worse.

July 23

The weather sucks. Matt and I were forced off the river today and then our tent nearly got flooded. Where is the sun?

— Megan

Megan visits with Ruby elder Nora Kangis during our short stay in the village. Her subsistence diet of fish, game, and berries keeps her healthy. "I can't eat anything artificial," she says. "The doctor said I'll live to be a hundred."

We accept an invitation to stay at the Shaw family's cabin downriver from the village of Ruby. Nestled back in the spruce next to a clear, gurgling creek, the cabin is a cozy retreat from the wet, windy day out on the Yukon River.

Ruby is a rough-cut gem in Alaska. Like many villages along the Yukon, it pops up out of nowhere and sits perched over the river in approval. Gold strikes on nearby Ruby and Long Creeks brought a thousand prospectors to the small Athabascan village in the early 1900s. Mining was a major economic force up until the 1950s. Now the 170 residents have turned back to the land and river to make ends meet. The sun is shining again and we take advantage, barbecuing chicken and potatoes over a fire. We've pitched our tent in a campground with a covered pavilion just a few feet from the boat ramp. Aluminum riverboats start to arrive down on the banks, bringing in the daily catch from subsistence nets and fish wheels. As if on cue, the whole village turns out to help prepare hundreds of salmon for the smokehouse. A couple more boats arrive, the whining of their engines cutting out just before they slide up onto the gravel banks. They bring a more precious cargo: village friends from downriver who have traveled up for a weekend visit. The scene is reminiscent of another time and place, when river travel was a social or practical event, not just an adventure.

We leave Ruby on a cold misty day. Luckily, as we're getting ready to push off, we meet Randy Shaw. He and his wife, Lucy, moved to Ruby a few years earlier from outside Alaska. "Sight unseen," he says. During the summer they run canoe and kayak trips up and down the Yukon. We're happy to hear that tourists get to experience this part of the river. Randy tells us that, in the winter, he runs dogs with a friend. "Just getting by, living the simple life," he says. He then tells us about his cabin downriver. He looks at the sky, then back at us, and says we are welcome to stay there if the weather turns. "Just look for the pink flamingos," he laughs. Shaw also recommends that we stop and visit with his downriver neighbor, John Stam. We have never met Stam, but that's how the river is. Travelers love to stop and get a break and most people enjoy getting visitors.

Stam is a character. He homesteaded on the Yukon River years ago and his property looks like a village itself. There are several buildings, boats, and the hum of a generator. He also has several large windmills generating power. As soon as we dock, Stam comes out from his cabin and waves us up. On the river it never takes long to get acquainted. Immediately we swap stories about our adventures, and Matt and I listen like children as Stam shares his stories of trapping in the winter and canning salmon in the summer. Whenever Matt and I are feeling proud and tough for doing

August 2

River looked dismal this morning heading out of Ruby: rain, wind, cold. Not a day to be spending ten hours in a canoe. Stopped to have a long lunch and a bit of rhubarb wine with river local John Stam before continuing to the Shaws' cabin.

—Matt

It might look simple, but the Shaws' cabin was our equivalent of a Yukon River Hilton.

81

Traditional Athabascan beadwork on moosehide by Lucy Whalen of Galena. Whalen was preparing gifts for an upcoming potlatch to commemorate the death of her mother.

this trip, all we need to do is meet the people who live on the river all year. Their stories of surviving and living a subsistence lifestyle make our stories pale by comparison. John offers us some of his homemade rhubarb wine. That, plus the pilot bread and smoked salmon, warm me right up.

We see the bright pink flamingos soon after leaving Stam's. With only one small cabin, Shaw's property is the opposite of Stam's. A freshwater creek runs alongside it. A closer look reveals a basket filled with cold beer and soda. A metal water tank is perched 10 feet in the air over a wood-burning barrel to provide an outdoor shower. We head into the cabin and find a comfortable bed covered in mosquito netting.

"Another night in a luxury hotel," I tell myself with a big smile. We settle in with some books from Shaw's small library. One is a book of tales from the Yukon River. Some of the people featured in the book we've already met, like Stan Zuray and Charlie Campbell. I relish every word. In the last few days I've found myself enjoying our adventure more and more. My fears are fading, and life on the river is more enchanting every day. For the first time during our trip, I pray for a rainy day so we can stay put at Shaw's.

The Yukon grows wider with every day's travel. It will now take us about an hour to ferry across if need be. We're thankful that all the villages in this region are on the north bank. As we near Galena, the village after Ruby, the river's mighty current swings us around turn after turn, as the water works away at cutbanks more than a hundred feet high. Each corner displays a mosaic of earth tones stratified in the silty soil and exposed by the river. Layers of permafrost—a lens of underground ice that is insulated from the summer heat—sometimes lie exposed, melting in the July sun. As the river carves and the ice melts, large chunks of earth plunge into the Yukon with a tsunami-like roar interrupting the silence. We watch from a safe distance as entire lengths of riverbank fall into the water, trees and all.

From nearly a mile away, we get our first glimpse of Galena, the largest community on the middle river, with over 700 full-time residents. Established in 1918 from a collection of fish camps, Galena has become the transportation center of the middle Yukon River.

Galena native Lucy Whalen has been extremely busy this summer preparing for her mother's potlatch. In the Athabascan culture, a potlatch is a large ceremony to commemorate major life events, in this instance the death of Lucy's mother.

Yukon River artist Wolf Hebel shows us his antler carvings at his log cabin studio in Ruby. Originally from Germany, he combs the wilderness hunting for wood, antler, and fossils to use in his sculptures.

Sometimes the preparations can take years. Lucy is one of twelve children and all of them are planning on attending the memorial. She invites us into her single-room home to watch her bead. In addition to a bed, the 10-by-12-foot room has a television and a radio. At the moment, both are turned on. Lucy tells us to sit down and stops sewing. She slowly pulls out bags of her homemade treasures: intricate pillows, gloves, earrings. Many of the items are worth several hundred dollars apiece. They will not be sold, she says, but given away at the potlatch as a way to say thanks to those who helped with her mom's funeral. It is also a way for Lucy to honor her mother, and—I think—forget about the pain of losing her.

After a few cloudy days, the sun returns without warning and we marvel at the luck of another hot day on the river. In a few days the yellows and browns of fall will slowly transform the hillsides. Floating through the beauty of the Yukon, I am finally beginning to understand why Matt loves Alaska so much and why I am falling more in love with it as well. The attraction to the river and its landscape is instantaneous, like a high-school crush. The beauty takes your breath away and the quiet humbles you in a way you hadn't ever thought possible. Strangely, I am imagining what it would be like to have our own cabin on the Yukon. Stranger yet, I'm beginning to enjoy the idea. We take turns pointing out one perfect spot after the next to build our Yukon retreat.

The harsh autumn winds catch up to us in the village of Koyukuk. We seek shelter against the gusts in our tent. During the afternoon, several people stop by to talk about the tragic death of a longtime Galena resident the night before. Well-known bar owner Archie Thurmond, his wife, and their grandchildren were traveling back from a softball tournament in Huslia on the Koyukuk River, when their boat caught fire. Everyone but Archie was able to swim to safety.

Life on the river is hard, and even a day of play can turn tragic. We are aware of that each day as we set out on the river, no matter how calm it is. There are risks, and we are taking them. These thoughts run through my mind as I look out on the ever-growing expanse of the Yukon. The horizon is nothing but water, shimmering in the sun like a great inland sea. It is here that our route turns south into the last part of our journey, the lower Yukon. The end is finally in sight, even if it still lies over 500 miles off in the distance. If the first two sections of the Yukon are any indication, it's not going to be easy.

August 3

This morning the sun was shining and the wind moderate. Matt and I had hoped to hit Galena in 6.5 hours. 8 hours later we landed. The last five miles dragged on and on. A bacon, lettuce and tomato sandwich at the local restaurant made up for it. We found an okay campsite in front of an old boarded-up trailer home. Actually it's a dump, but we don't care anymore. Every day of travel seems to wear us out more and more.

— Megan

The community of Ruby turns out to welcome friends and family from downriver to the Athabascan village. Visitors arrive by boat or plane and stay a couple days, a couple weeks, or months at a time.

PART III

KWIKPAK

Koyukuk to St. Marys, Alaska

*Facing the usual gale, we drifted slowly down the river to Kaltag, where
the south bank becomes a simple flat plateau, though the north bank is
high and even mountainous for more than four hundred miles farther.
It seemed not improbable that this had been the Yukon's ancient mouth,
when the river flowed over all the flat plain down to the sea. Certainly the
deposit from the river is now filling in the eastern shores of Bering's Sea.
Navigators about the coast say it is dangerous for vessels of any
considerable draught to sail within fifty or a hundred miles of land near
the Yukon's mouth, and every storm lashes the sea into a muddy froth.*

— Lt. Frederick Schwatka, 1883

As we float out from the confluence of the Koyukuk and Yukon
Rivers, we feel very small. Straight off our bow, the wide expanse of
water is endless. Here, in the middle of a large bend, the Yukon's channel
turns south toward the villages of Nulato and Kaltag, but we might as
well be paddling into the ocean.

The boundary marking the edges of Indian and Eskimo traditional
homelands along this stretch of the Yukon was never clearly defined, but
each group fought to protect its hunting and fishing grounds, and trade
as well as war is part of both groups' oral histories. Yup'ik Eskimos are

*The Yukon River fills our horizon off the bow of
Lucille as we make our turn south at the village of Koyukuk.*

Some of the first Russian explorers of this region are buried in the cemetery overlooking Nulato, Alaska. The Athabascan village was the scene of much fighting between the Russian traders and area Natives.

present all the way up to the Koyukuk Valley. But not until much lower on the river would we find the stronghold of Yup'ik culture, where the Yukon was named *Kwikpak*, or "great river."

"I knew it was wide, but I didn't think we would notice it so soon," Matt says, standing up to get a good look at what's in store. What we first see with our eyes, we quickly begin to feel in the boat as *Lucille* bobs in the large windblown swells coming upriver. Nulato is just 18 river-miles away, but we feel timid and exposed on this vast section of open water. A stiff headwind lets us know it is going to be a long day.

"Let's just stay close to shore," I suggest in my best positive voice.

"Nah, let's try and ferry across," Matt says sarcastically, trying to make light of the situation. I force myself to laugh and grab my paddle tight as we inch *Lucille* as close to the gravel banks as possible without grinding her hull on the rocks. As we predicted, the winds increase as we make our way into the bend. The small rocky banks give way to towering craggy cliffs that drop vertically into the water. Waves that were just lapping at our bow now smash into the side of *Lucille*. We decide to head for shore. Heavy surf picks us up like a Dixie Cup and drops our 1,000-pound load hard on a rocky beach. Wave after wave dumps over our gunwales as we catch our breath. But there is no relaxing today and soon we head out again. Five miles into the day's journey and we're both exhausted, fighting the turbulent water.

"I think we should stop," Matt says, his voice actually trembling.

I turn and see that he is serious, scanning the shore for a place to pull out.

"I just can't control the boat anymore," he says.

I begin scanning the shore as well, but the steep bluffs that plunge into the river offer no refuge. I look miles across the river to the other side of the Yukon. A tree-lined shore there looks like an option, but ferrying across is not.

"Let's just stay close to shore and push on as far as we can," I say doubtfully, as another series of waves rock our canoe. Matt says nothing and keeps paddling. *Eighteen miles, is it too much to ask for?* I keep these thoughts to myself.

The continuous headwind fuels our tempers as we struggle for each and every mile of progress. It's been a long time since Matt and I have snapped at each other, but our frustration mounts with each crashing swell. My arms feel like they're about

All manner of watercraft could be found on the Yukon by 1906, from paddle-wheelers, to traditional birch-bark canoes, to flat-bottom boats. [PHOTO BY CLARENCE LEROY ANDREWS: ALASKA STATE LIBRARY, PCA #45-628]

August 7

It's awful, but Nulato is only 18 miles and Matt and I feel we can make it. We are burnt out after 5 miles and the waves are huge and dangerous. Matt is as frustrated and as tired as I am. We pull off at a fish camp and take a break. We are really scared. Matt says he just can't control the boat in the waves. He thinks we should stop. I urge him on though, and we paddle forward.

— Megan

to fall off from the endless hours of paddling. At any minute, a wave could bury us in a million gallons of muddy water. It takes us eight long hours, but we finally reach the landing in Nulato. Once on the beach, we just sit there, our nerves completely frazzled. Both of us stare at the Yukon wide-eyed. Like an animal of prey, the river seems to be hunting us. We both admit that we don't know how many more days like this we can take. I look up a small hill and notice a gravesite perched over the village. It's an ominous sight.

ORIGINALLY A TRADING SITE between Athabascans and Iñupiat Eskimos from the Kobuk River, Nulato is now home to about 320 permanent residents. In the early 1980s, the village began moving up from the river's edge to a new town site in the surrounding hills. Years of flooding were beginning to wear on people. We notice a new subdivision being built in the distance and decide to take a walk. The homes on the banks of the river are crafted mostly from logs, but the newer homes are built with wood siding. Tribal chief Peter Demoski says that providing affordable housing for residents is only one benefit of the project. He says the construction creates jobs, which in turn creates hope, something Demoski says younger rural residents need. Modern homes with modern amenities appeal to younger generations living in the Bush.

"They might just stick around," Demoski says.

But even with the incentives of indoor plumbing and Maytag dishwashers, many of the village's elders remain in their almost century-old homes next to the river. There is no spiritual division among residents, but the geographical division symbolizes a dilemma faced by many in rural Alaska, the old versus the new. As this village compromises to stay alive, I can't help but think back on the many villages we've visited that seem to be on the brink of dying.

The weather takes a turn for the worse in Nulato, and we find ourselves spending four days camped in our tent. Each morning we wake up expecting to see the river calmed by a good night's rest, and each morning we're disappointed to see the waves looking larger than the day before. By the fifth morning the four-foot swells have died down and so has the wind. The river is rough, but we have to get moving.

We quickly pack the boat and reluctantly push off, knowing the conditions are far from ideal.

"We'll stay close to shore and get off if it gets any worse," Matt says.

But no sooner does he say "worse" then a gust of wind lifts the front of *Lucille* sharply out of the water. We immediately check the shore for a place to land.

"Look over there." Matt yells. "It looks like a fish camp. I'm sure we can stay there."

"I hope so," I yell back, helping Matt turn the boat. We paddle furiously to keep *Lucille* upright. From Nulato's shoreline, the river looked small and wavy, but now that we're on the water, the swells are enormous. We finally get to the camp and pull into a makeshift boat ramp. The place is deserted, but signs of at least one recent visitor are everywhere.

"Wow, this is a big grizzly," Matt says, tracing his hand over the large paw print. I look down to see for myself.

"We shouldn't stay here," I say.

"No, probably not," Matt agrees, "but for now we have to. Let's have lunch and see if it calms down."

Matt walks back to the canoe to unload some gear, but I wander around, intrigued by the deserted camp. Rotted salmon hang from the skeleton of an old

Ryan Madros is hard at work building a house for the NAHASDA project in the village of Nulato. The subsidized program provides jobs and new housing for the villagers.

smokehouse. I can't tell if they are month-old leftovers or year-old leftovers. The smell flushes my nostrils and I place my hand over my nose. I turn to look for Matt.

"This is a death trap for sure!" I yell. "We can't stay here. We just can't—it's way too dangerous." It's cool out today, but I feel the sweat trickle down my back.

"Calm down," Matt says grabbing my hand. "Let's take a look around before getting all worked up."

It is too late. The smell alone has me in a tizzy.

"We've definitely had better camps," Matt says casually. Grabbing my arm he leads me to where he's already started a campfire. I follow, realizing Matt is the only thing between me and a grizzly bear who for the time being, also calls this camp home. The fire relaxes me and I get out a book. In no time we're lying back against a log reading and drinking tea. Periodically, I sit up and glance in all four directions. The spot isn't all that bad, as long as I don't see that grizzly.

With nowhere else to go and the wind only picking up, we make camp and hang out. Not just one day but two full days. In my boredom I clean up around the camp, as if the owner might return at any moment. I locate what was once the kitchen area and set up our stove. To pass the time, Matt and I play cards hour after hour, just waiting for the river to calm.

Bear tracks slice into the muddy banks along the Yukon River just a few feet from our camp. Even though we watched dozens of bears from afar and encountered signs of their passing, we did not have one close encounter during our 90-day voyage.

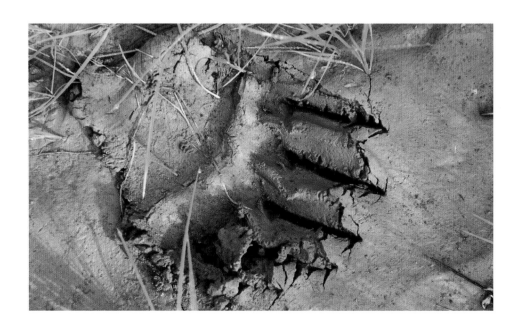

It is now mid-August, nearly three months into our journey, and we're trapped in a rotting fish camp. I wonder what will happen if we get stuck here. I cross my arms around my chest and shiver in the cold wind. I've taken to wearing my winter cap nonstop. Looking out on the Yukon, I watch as huge waves crest the shore, resembling an ocean more than a river. By our estimates we should reach the Bering Sea in less than two weeks—if we get two weeks of good travel days. Lately, getting two good travel days in a row has been tough. Though neither of us is saying it, getting to the end is more difficult than we ever imagined.

"Tomorrow we leave no matter what and get to a better camp," Matt says.

"I'm okay," I try to reassure him. But I'm ready to move on.

The next morning, the water has calmed a little, but the sky is black with rain. The temperature is a windy 45 degrees. We pack the boat quietly and efficiently, determined to make it a few more miles. Our short-sleeved T-shirts are packed deep in the bottom of our dry-bags. For the last week, we've been wearing layers of clothes—fleece jackets, gloves, hats. If fall isn't here, it's pretty close.

"Ready?" Matt asks.

"Ready!" I say, smiling back at him.

At the beginning of our trip, Matt's confidence made up for my lack of confidence. Now, the playing field is level. We are literally and figuratively in the same boat. We can tell immediately that the river is not going to give us a break this day. At each bend, the eddies kick up water and twist *Lucille*'s bow faster than we can get our paddles turned around. It's not easy, but Matt manages to steer the boat.

With resolve in my eyes, I glance back at him. "Good job!" I yell. We paddle hard, fighting for every mile, finally reaching a small side channel that should bring us right into Kaltag. Surprisingly, the water is calming. A light drizzle fills the air, but the wind is no longer forcing its way upriver. For us, that is the only incentive we need to keep paddling.

It is the break we've been waiting for. For the first time in weeks, suddenly the Yukon is glassy smooth. The fierce headwind that's been with us since Galena has shut down. I don't even notice the steady rain soaking through my windbreaker.

The day just gets better as a generous tailwind starts pushing *Lucille* toward our goal. After weeks of stressful hours in the canoe, we're finally able to relax and enjoy the hidden beauty of the lower Yukon. It seems that just as we are tiring of the river's

August 11

It looks decent, and Matt and I decide Kaltag is reachable. But of course Mother Nature has other plans, and two hours into our journey we are forced off the river. Fortunately we are in striking distance of a deserted fish camp. Unfortunately when we arrive we notice all of the rotting fish and salmon strips. It's buggy and smelly and Matt is freaking out. The grizzly tracks all over freak me out.

— Megan

August 16,
Thursday, Day 69
Blackburn Island,
Alaska

　Just floated along today, talking and drinking hot tea. This is how I had envisioned our canoe trip. Magnificent mountains stand between the ocean and us. They are bald and gently rolling; ancient looking.
　Longtime Galena resident Archie Thurmond was recently buried in the village across the river. "I wouldn't mind being buried out here," said Megan. Maybe this, right here on the Yukon River, is as close as one can walk next to God without dying.

—Matt

scenery, it changes. Long stretches of vast mudflats surround us one moment and steep lush valleys the next. During one particularly breathtaking spot upriver from Grayling, the Yukon moves through a steep and narrow canyon. A small waterfall cascades down the lush green wall. Once again the river proves how quickly it can change from a harsh unforgiving place to one of overwhelming beauty.

I feel Matt steer the boat toward shore and turn to see what he's up to.

"I have to go to the bathroom," he says.

I look to the shore and see a small beach. We pull the canoe up and Matt walks into the trees. I notice some bear scat and footprints almost immediately. Though I rarely touch our handgun, I have a bad feeling about this spot and reach for the waterproof carrying case. I hadn't planned to take it out, but when I suddenly hear rustling coming from the bushes in the opposite direction of Matt, I unlatch the case and cautiously grab the .44 magnum.

"Matt?" I whisper loudly. He doesn't answer and I begin to panic. *How far could he have gone?* I ask myself. In a few seconds I've convinced myself he's been eaten by a bear.

"Matt!" I say again, this time more loudly. There is still no answer. Sitting on *Lucille*'s bow I peer from side to side, my hands wrapped around the revolver's grip. It's funny, after weeks of not worrying, a small spot of scat has me terrified. Suddenly I hear a large crunching sound from the woods and point the gun in that direction.

"What the . . . ?" Matt screams, when he sees me pointing the gun at him.

"Where were you?!" I shout. "I've been sitting here for 10 minutes—I thought you got mauled by a bear!"

Just as I think he's about to yell at me, instead he breaks into a fit of laughter.

"That's probably the funniest thing I have ever seen," he says.

I fail to see the humor. *He's lucky I didn't shoot*, I tell myself, placing the gun carefully back in its case.

A STRONG TAILWIND has been with us for over a day now, and we've been taking full advantage. Lost in the joy of not fighting a headwind, Matt and I neglect to see what is staring us straight in the face: several dark clouds. We feel the rain first and then, out of nowhere, a small breeze brushes past our cheeks. Not wanting to jinx our string of good luck, we both keep quiet, hoping to silence the inevitable. In a matter of minutes there is no denying it: our enemy, the headwind, is back.

"Let's get a little closer to land," Matt says.

I agree with a strong paddle to the right. The waves start small, but quickly progress to three-foot swells. The cursing behind me coming from Matt signals that our brief leisurely visit with the lower Yukon is over.

"Hard right," Matt yells.

I give it my all, but the wind is unrelenting.

"Let's get her into shore," he commands.

I look to the west bank. Thick brush extends right down to the river.

"What shore?" I ask Matt. The bow of our boat crashes against the rolling white-caps. I can't believe how quickly the river changes. In all of our weeks of treacherous water, this is the worst. The storm we're in is fast and furious. A heavy torrential downpour washes across our faces, making it difficult to see.

"We got it," Matt encourages, his own panic revealed in his voice.

About two feet from shore, he jumps into the water with the bowline, pulling us to land. He grabs my hand and pulls me out of the canoe. We look around disheart-ened. There is hardly any place to stand, let alone pitch a tent. A throng of bad words coming from my normally calm partner is just one indication of a pretty bad sit-uation. Matt decides we are going to line our canoe down the bank in search of a clearing to set up our tent. Cold and soaked, I do as I'm told. It sounds easy enough, but trying to keep *Lucille* out in the water and not crashing into shore proves to be nearly impossible.

On the verge of tears, I decide on my own to walk into the river a little and use my arms to keep the boat from getting pushed onto the gravel bank with every wave. My left hand on the boat, my right holding the line, I have to run to keep up with Matt. Suddenly I fall face-first into the water. I'm afraid to let go of the line, and the boat drags me for a few feet before I get myself back up. Matt doesn't even notice. I feel the water rush into my tall rubber boots, my socks sucking in the cold moisture. Now I'm the one swearing. It was the first time my boots had failed me. I quickly think back to the day we bought them in Fairbanks.

"You want me to spend how much on these?" I gasped, holding the brown rub-ber boots. "These are the ugliest boots I've ever seen."

95

August 17

It is absolutely the most terrifying, cold, miserable experience so far on the trip. We line the boat around a corner and head for slough. We find a sandbar to camp on and there are bear marks all over the place, but we have no choice. I am finished. No more of this, it is no longer fun.

— Megan

"Meg, you need them to keep your feet warm and dry," Matt had said. "Trust me."

"Fine," I said, "but I want you to know I don't normally spend $100 on boots unless they are Italian leather."

Now, in the unforgiving waters of the Yukon, soaked to the bone, I laugh out loud at the absurdity of it all. The boots, my pea-green plastic rain gear, the snot running down my face. I was the farthest thing from the made-up little anchor that people saw on television.

"Why are you laughing?" Matt shouts back at me.

"Cause this sucks! If I don't laugh, I'll cry," I scream back.

"I think there's a clearing ahead where we can set up the tent," Matt says. "Just another mile or so."

When we finally get there, we are absolutely exhausted. The cold rain slaps our faces, reminding us that the punishment is not over yet. We look around to see that "the clearing" is thick with mud and full of tangled debris, left over from a large log jam. Worse yet, everywhere we look there are fresh bear tracks. There is no place to set up a tent.

"Could this day get any worse?" I say out loud, addressing the sky.

Matt studies our current position on the map and thinks that we might find a protected side slough just up ahead. The only catch is that we have run out of beach and will have to venture back onto the turbulent water. Since I'm not about to camp here, I agree to Matt's plan, no matter how perilous it might be. My thought processes are all but wiped out for the day.

Back in the canoe, I feel like my life is about to end at any moment. Shaking in the cold unrelenting rain, I paddle through crashing waves with a glazed look. Matt turns around every so often to see how I am doing.

"We're almost there, babe," he coaxes.

To where? To hell? I wonder. I paddle as if it is a reflex now. Before I know it, Matt has guided us into a very small muddy slough with an island full of goose poop. There is enough of a clearing for our tent, and a small logjam will provide plenty of wood for a fire. I stand around numb as Matt sets up the tent. I look down and immediately notice the tracks. Enormous grizzly prints make a deep indentation in the wet mud, the nails leaving an inch thick impression. They're clearly only minutes old. I feel dizzy and too tired to care. Matt rushes me, slightly hypothermic,

A houseboat makes its way up the Yukon on a windy afternoon near Nulato.

inside as soon as the tent is set up and pulls out some dry clothes. A small tear escapes my eye. I've been strong the entire trip, but today's ordeal is unraveling any amount of determination I have left.

"Meg, it's okay, we're going to be fine," Matt says. "I'm going to get a fire started and make some warm tea." His voice is much more soothing than an hour ago.

I lie down in the tent and change into dry clothes. *He'll never get a fire started*, I tell myself. The pouring rain has not stopped all afternoon. The tears come in a steady stream now, as I try to choke back the sobs. I'm battling with Mother Nature and she's winning. I don't know why I thought I could do this. Sensing my hopelessness, Matt helps me out of the tent to a makeshift shelter. Using our blue tarp, he's built an awning over a small campfire.

"How did you get a fire started?" I ask, looking at the soaking wet wood.

He grabs a small empty bottle that once held our reserve of gasoline, "It was for an emergency, and this is an emergency," Matt says smiling.

"What smells so good?" I ask, the tension somewhat diminishing.

"Pizza!" Matt says proudly, handing me a hot, steaming slice. I walk over to him and give him a hug. My darkest moment has come and gone. I am not convinced that I will go any farther than the next village with an airstrip, but once again, thanks to Matt, I feel a little sense of hope.

A TINY VILLAGE sitting in an immense landscape, Grayling is named after the creek at the south end of the town. There are about 160 full-time residents. We meet Wilfred Deacon almost immediately. He asks what we're doing. When we explain about our trip, he tells us that a lot of people quit here.

"The weather, the wind, the currents get even worse," he says, pointing downriver.

"Thanks a lot," Matt says. It was not what we wanted to hear after our experience the day before. The trip from "bear claw" island into Grayling was short and painless and made us feel better. Still, our cold, wet, and frustrating ordeal is fresh in our minds.

Matt begins to build a fire on Grayling's beach, and Wilfred takes off on his four-wheeler. A few minutes later, he returns with a huge red salmon and a bottle of lighter fluid. At first Matt is fine with Wilfred's help, until Wilfred decides to pour the entire bottle on an already raging fire.

"Whoa," Matt says, "I think that's good."

Smiling, he looks Wilfred over, slightly annoyed and slightly intrigued with the man who enjoys a fire as much as he does. After enjoying a little salmon with us, Wilfred abruptly takes off.

"Bye Mac," he yells. He apparently misheard Matt's name. We look at each other and laugh.

Ten minutes later Wilfred returns with some homemade donuts.

"My wife made these from scratch," he says proudly. "Cook she does—she's a great cook! She works at the store all day and cooks at night."

"What do you do, Wilfred?" I ask.

"My wife works," is his only response. Again Matt and I look at each other and smile. Wilfred is just the breath of fresh air that we need.

Later that night in our tent, we hear a four-wheeler outside.

"Hey Mac, how's it going?" we hear Wilfred shout through the tent fly.

Matt unzips the door. "Hey Wilfred," he says, "we're just getting ready to go to sleep."

◄ *Megan gives an impromptu cooking lesson to the Yup'ik children of Pilot Station on the lower Yukon River.*

Wilfred does not seem to care, however, and begins singing us to sleep. We break into a fit of laughter as he sings one off-key Hank Williams song after the next.

In the morning, a steady rain keeps us tucked warmly in our tent. Wilfred stops by repeatedly, singing more Hank Williams and bringing food. Each time he offers us a warm cabin to stay in. Each time Matt politely says no thank you.

"I would," he explains after Wilfred leaves, "but a day of Wilfred's singing could really do this trip in!"

After five days of tough travel and cold weather, nothing sounds better than a hot shower. Unfortunately, the washeteria in Grayling is under renovation, so we have to wait until Anvik, the next village downriver. The trip there is quick and—except for an exciting crossing of the Anvik River—pretty uneventful. Something we haven't seen in a long time is also present as we arrive: the sun.

We take a small slough into Anvik and set up camp on the front lawn of a gorgeous log church, part of the original Episcopal mission in Anvik. I look at the church and quickly reach for my copy of *Two in the Far North* by Margaret "Mardy"

► *The Episcopal Church overlooks the Anvik River in the village of Anvik, Alaska.*

Murie. It's about her adventures in Alaska with her husband, Olaus Murie, a biologist who surveyed the Arctic. I had not heard about the book until I started planning the Yukon trip. Someone gave me a copy as a gift. Once I began reading the book, I understood why. Mardy Murie also spends months traveling the Yukon with Olaus.

On bad days I would often reach for the book and be comforted by Mardy's adventures and sometimes her struggles. Today I reach for my book for another reason. The church we are sleeping in front of is the same log church where Olaus and Mardy were married on August 19, 1924. Coincidentally, it's August 20, 2001—almost exactly 77 years since that day.

"Can you believe it?" I ask Matt.

"Yeah, I can believe it," he says smugly, grabbing me and leading me in an impromptu dance. His hand secured tightly around my waist, I revel in the simple joy of dancing on the banks of the Yukon River with no music.

As Matt turns me in circles, I think about all the fancy weddings we're missing this summer back in the suburbs of Chicago. For some reason a dozen of my friends decided this was the summer to tie the knot. I look down at my filthy clothes and brown rubber boots and smile. My hair is tied up in a bun and tucked under a blue bandana. If they could see me now, they would laugh. I look up at Matt. He tilts his head down and softly kisses my forehead. I hug his waist, thankful I'm nowhere near a country club in Chicago.

Later that evening, Matt sets up his tripod and takes several pictures of the church. I love watching him work. There is a sparkle in his eyes when the light is just right and his picture so clear. After the difficulty of last week's tough travel, tonight I remember why I am doing all of this. Matt's photography is what brought us out here in the first place, and I have taken great pleasure in watching him fulfill a dream. There is never a guarantee that anyone will buy his photographs, but for Matt, every picture is valuable. His passion for his work is enviable.

Matt and I walk up to the laundromat first thing in the morning and get our chores done. We both cringe after taking cold showers. As I wait for the laundry to dry, Matt says he's going to get a head start on breaking down camp. I let him go, not realizing how difficult it's going to be to carry the clean laundry by myself. In the middle of rearranging the bags for the third time, a woman on a four-wheeler stops right in front of me.

August 21

The rapids are more
than Matt and I can
handle. Suddenly we
find ourselves in a
mile of choppy, choppy
water. Water flows over
the top of the canoe and
the sides and I begin to
get hysterical. Matt
tries to placate me.
With just three miles
left in our day, disaster
seems imminent. We
are both exhausted
from our nine-hour
day. We ponder what
looks like the end of our
journey. Suddenly
Matt says, "Well,
Whitehorse to Holy
Cross is a great journey."
"Yes, it is," I say. But
I know it is not what we
set out to do.

— Megan

"Hi, where ya from?" she shouts over the drone of the machine.

"Fairbanks," I answer.

"What are you doing here?" she asks.

I tell her about our trip and she looks surprised.

"The whole river?" she asks in disbelief.

"The whole river," I say, not quite believing it myself.

"My name is Daisy," she says. "It looks like you could use a ride."

The laundry bags heavy on my arms, I say thanks and hop onto the back of her four-wheeler. At first I don't notice the thick-rimmed glasses she's wearing, but now, sitting on the metal grate behind her seat, and traveling at 40 miles an hour, I'm beginning to wonder if she can see at all. Daisy veers from side to side, speeding down the road. I try to juggle the bags while clutching the bars so I don't fall off. My legs flail in the air as the dust flares up behind the wheels and into my eyes. Daisy pumps the gas and speeds up, flying through Anvik like pollen on a blustery spring day. I watch as a small group of pedestrians gets out of her way. She waves and flashes the group a big smile. As we zoom past, the group points at me and laughs. Either I look as stupid as I think I look, or they know something about Daisy I don't. I suddenly realize that it doesn't matter if I am on the river or in town; my chances of dying in the Bush are just as high.

"Th-thanks for the ride," I muster, as Daisy lets me off a few feet from our tent.

Without saying good-bye, she's off, spitting dust all over my clean clothes. Matt walks over to my side and we watch the four-wheeler swerve through town.

"Who's that?" Matt asks, dusting dirt off my clothes.

"Her name is Daisy, but she drives like Dale Earnhardt," I laugh.

OUR LAST SUPPLY of food waits for us at the Holy Cross post office. We are picking it up on a morning in late August. Inside one of the boxes is a bottle of champagne to celebrate our arrival at the Bering Sea. The thought of not popping it makes my heart sink. The last few weeks of travel have tired us out, and our short trip from Anvik to Holy Cross was not easy. As we pitch the tent in Holy Cross, Matt and I talk over our options, finally admitting that we might not be traveling any farther.

We fall asleep in despair. But at three in the morning, I wake to go to the bathroom and find relief somewhere I did not expect. Up above, a gorgeous display of northern lights shimmers across the dark sky. It's the first time I've seen them now that the days are growing shorter.

"Matt, Matt, wake up," I whisper. "The northern lights are out." Matt peeks his head out of the side of the tent.

"Oh, wow, they're really crackling," he says. Looking into the sky I feel the pull of northern Alaska again. The aurora borealis streams through the stars, its haunting flares of light luring us back to the land we've called home all summer long. I glance at the Yukon and see a perfectly clear reflection of green and blue lights dancing on

Like children everywhere, the kids at Holy Cross hang out together to pass a summer's day.

the glassy surface of the water. We stand in awe as the earth and sky join forces, feeling the precious, unmistakable beauty found only in the great north. Matt puts his hand on my shoulder and I know tomorrow we're getting back in *Lucille* and continuing on. We have no choice, the end is simply too close.

The sun and heat in Holy Cross follow us downriver on the way to Russian Mission. We're able to relax and float, rather than constantly paddle *Lucille*. In the evening we decide to camp on a magnificent sandbar a mile upriver from the village. The sun sets over the Yukon–Kuskokwim Delta with a fury that night. Low clouds reflect bright pinks and yellows across the river. Like the double rainbow back in Circle, something is trying to keep us on the river.

The original Russian Orthodox Church at Russian Mission, Alaska. Most communities along the lower Yukon River were shaped by traveling missionaries.

KWIKPAK

The dilapidated roof of the old Russian Orthodox Church peeks out over Russian Mission, a Yup'ik village originally known as Ikogmiut. In 1851, Father Jacob Netsvetov, a missionary of Aleut and Russian ancestry, arrived here to evangelize the local Natives. In 1994, the church canonized the Alaskan priest; today he is venerated worldwide as St. Jacob. This village was also the site of the first Russian-American Company trading post on the Yukon River. Here is yet another place that was forever changed by the influence of non-Natives through trade and religion.

Our gear is taking a beating as the sand of the lower river turns into a deep, sticky mud. Setting up the tent is becoming increasingly difficult. After months of constant use, the zippers are failing and the outside of our portable "summer cottage" is filthy. The lower Yukon is a series of muddy sandbars and a thick layer of silt is everywhere. I think back on how long it took us to choose just the right shelter. Matt had insisted that we bring a spacious four-person tent.

"It's going to be our home for three months," he said then, passing on the two-person model a salesperson was trying to sell us. I didn't realize how important a role it would play in our journey. Now I know. At the end of a long day, the tent protects us from the weather and the bugs. On rainy days, or lately during rainy weeks, there is always plenty of room and comfort. I've grown to love the tent and hate to see it fall apart.

"Grab me the duct tape," Matt says one evening, trying to fasten the tent door to the tent side.

"I don't think that's going to work," I say, doubting this particular use of the wide, silvery tape that's used everywhere in Alaska. Quickly rolling his eyes, Matt sets out to prove me wrong. Doubting duct tape in Alaska is like doubting your own name. With fierce determination, he grabs the side of the tent and the door of the tent, pulling them together with one hand. With his other hand, he tries to tape them together. The first section goes all right, but as he moves up the zipper, and pulls the two sides together, the portion below that he's just taped comes undone. Biting on his tongue, sweat dripping from his forehead, he retapes it, only to have the same thing happen four more times. I watch in amusement for about an hour before grabbing my bag and digging deep for a needle and thread.

"I think this will work better," I offer quietly. Even worse than doubting duct tape is being correct about its inadequacies.

August 22

We saw the northern lights last night. Alaska toys with me. For all its tough exterior walls, its calm serene beauty draws me in. The previous afternoon the river was mean and nasty. Now tonight, she gleams like glass. The northern lights and a clear starry night give the appearance of calm. The river calls me back. "Come on, you can do it, see . . . I'll be calm for you."

— Megan

August 24,
Friday, Day 77
Tucker's Crossing,
Alaska

We're sitting pretty on a
sandy island about five
miles before Russian
Mission. Fire's going and
dinner has been served.
Nice cup of wine while
we watch rainbows
come and go over the
mountains. The Yukon is
glassy smooth tonight.
The river is so huge
down here; some sections
are like paddling an
ocean with no land on
the horizon.
　　　　　　　—Matt

An evening rainbow frames the rugged tundra slopes of Mount Chiniklik and Dogfish Mountain upriver from the village of Russian Mission.

August 29,
Wednesday, Day 82
Yukon Islands, Alaska

I call these the Yukon
Islands as the river's
name is printed across
them on the map. Our
Swiss friends came
paddling around the
corner in their two
inflatable crafts and had
trouble getting off the
water. We watched
them struggle across the
river getting their outfit
up on top of a six-foot-
tall cut bank. I was
thankful for our spot on
the island.

   Wind and rain
continued through the
day. Was really hoping
to finish the four hours
to the next village today,
but it was bad out there.
Maybe in the morning.
                    —Matt

About two dozen small children greet us as we pull into Pilot Station. Matt is unsure what to do as the curious little children follow us around. On the other hand, I see a big opportunity and engage the children in a game.

"Who wants to help unload our canoe?" I ask the staring faces. Every one of their hands shoots up in the air. In a matter of seconds our entire boat is empty and the tent set up. The giggling children hang around for hours, watching us cook up some red sauce and pasta. Hours after the sunset, we hear a bell and suddenly the children disappear.

"Curfew," Matt says with relief.

Early the next morning we slip out of Pilot Station. The heat wave is over, and it's nasty outside. Cold, windy rain dampens our spirits and the river is working itself into a frenzy. We make a quick crossing to an island across the way and decide it's not safe to travel any farther. We set up camp, not knowing if it's going to be our last.

IT'S DAY THREE on the island across from Pilot Station and Matt figures the Bering Sea is just 24 hours of travel away—about 100 miles. We can get there in three decent-weather days. It's now August 29, and we'd hoped to be off the river by September 1. No such luck.

We sit at our campfire and watch as a motorboat struggles to cross the water. We're stunned by the driver's courage. The waves on the river are the biggest we've seen so far. Matt estimates the swells to be anywhere from five to seven feet. Watching the bow of the motorboat lift and crash into the water, I don't doubt him anymore. We're only certain of one thing: we are not going anywhere until the waves calm.

"If we get a break, we can paddle downriver to Pitkas Point and fly out from there," Matt says, plotting a worst-case scenario. It is frustrating to be so close and so very far away from the end.

On the fifth morning on the island, the water calms just enough to allow for travel. If it were any other point in our trip, we'd probably stay on shore, but four days stranded on an island in cold, rainy weather is enough for both of us. We stay close to shore and fight the strong headwind with determination. Pitkas Point is a few miles away and reaching the small village today is our only goal. At first the wind and waves are more of an annoyance than anything else, but once we leave a small channel and the river opens up, the waves toss *Lucille* around. Matt and I feel as if the canoe is going to capsize at any moment. As our panic begins to rise from within, a motorboat suddenly shows up. The two people in it tell us to get to land. But they don't offer us a ride.

"You can make it to Pitkas," the driver says. "It's just over there." Matt and I look in the direction he's pointing and see several small buildings. Neither of us can imagine continuing, but the option of staying camped on the shore for another week is not appealing.

"Let's go for it, Meg," Matt says. Not wanting to disappoint, I go along with the plan. Fear grips my body, and I do a mental check of all my safety gear. I make sure my life vest is fastened tight and my emergency fanny pack is strapped to my waist. I glance at my sneakers. Good, they're double-knotted. We don't like to travel with our boots on in bad weather. If we go over, the boots will fill with water and weigh us down.

August 29

Our tent zippers have had it, kind of like me. Though not a major catastrophe, we rely on our tent and could not travel without it. The bugs and the weather would destroy us. Matt tried to fix one door with duct tape. He failed at fixing the zippers, but gave me a good laugh.

— Megan

High winds pin us down for four days near the end of our 2,000-mile journey. We make the best of being stranded on a small island just outside of Pilot Station.

Curious village children turn out
on the beach when we arrive at
the Yup'ik village of Pilot Station.
The kids eagerly help unload
Lucille, set up camp, and gather
a pile of driftwood.

During the previous century, children from around the Yukon–Kuskokwim Delta were sent to boarding school at the Catholic mission in St. Marys. Today the village acts as a regional hub for all transportation and commerce on the lower river.

"I'm ready if you are," I say, smiling back at Matt. I look across the great expanse of river. Here the Andreafsky River flows into the Yukon. The force of the two rivers meeting pummels *Lucille* forward. I feel the water come over the side of the boat, and paddle harder. We are now fighting six- and seven-foot swells.

"It's like the ocean," Matt screams.

"I would never do this on an ocean," I scream back, without turning to look at him.

We surf into the shore of Pitkas Point on a large wave, relief washing over us. We're sitting in the canoe, dazed, when out of nowhere a little girl with blonde hair appears on the beach.

"You guys want to come up for pancakes?" she asks. "My dad says it's okay." I look back at Matt and he's already nodding his head up and down. Like an angel, Jenna Fabich offers us more than a hot plate of food, she's the light at the end of a very long tunnel. Though we hope the weather might break, we're not counting on it.

Len and Jeanie Fabich, Jenna's parents, offer us a home-cooked breakfast and listen attentively as we recall the day's harrowing journey. Len talks about how he saw us from his kitchen window bobbing around in the water.

"I couldn't believe anyone would be out in that water," he says laughing. I gulp down a pancake. I can't believe we were out there either. Len explains that we can fly our gear and canoe back from the airstrip there. He says it as if he knows even before we do that we're not going any farther.

I look at Matt, expecting to see a face of disappointment, but instead he's smiling. "Thanks, Len. That sounds good," he says, reaching for my hand. I squeeze his hand in agreement. Our journey down the Yukon is over—just 60 miles shy of the Bering Sea. It seems appropriate that another kind Yukon River family is there to cushion the fall.

Two days later, we load *Lucille* into the back of an air-cargo transportation pickup truck. A cargo plane will fly her back to Anchorage with all of our gear. I feel funny sending her off. She's been holding us together for much of the trip. Letting *Lucille* go is like letting go of our dream to reach the Bering Sea. Matt and I watch as the truck pulls away, *Lucille*'s bow hanging out the back end. Her body is bruised with dirt and battered with dents. Bruised and battered, like our egos.

Our heads hanging low, Matt and I walk down to the river. The weather is only getting worse, and we wonder if we will even be able to fly out the next day. The mudflats of the lower Yukon are gold and brown as the cold arctic wind grips the Delta. It's now September 5, a week later than we expected to be out here. I have to be back at my job soon.

"It was awesome," Matt says, putting his arm around me, staring into the great expanse of water.

"But we didn't make it," I say sadly.

"It doesn't matter—it was awesome," Matt says. "We got to spend three months canoeing the Yukon River—to see parts of Alaska most people only dream about. And the people, Meg, think of all the amazing people we met."

Matt looks my way. "But most of all, we did it together," he says. "How many couples can say that?"

I look up at Matt and my heart jumps just as it did three long months earlier, when we first put *Lucille* in the water at Lake Laberge. Our adventure may be over, but our journey together is truly just beginning.

September 4

After three days trapped on an island, Matt and I made a mad dash for Pitkas Point. Another terrifying journey, but our last. We have decided to fly out of St. Marys. We talked about continuing on, but the weather is not going to get much better and we have had about all we can take. So close, but not close enough.

— Megan

EPILOGUE

AT THE MOUTH OF THE GREAT RIVER

*The spruce and poplar disappeared now, and low willows took their place,
though plenty of wood still abounded in immense drifts on the upstream
ends of the numerous islands. Near Andreavsky begins the delta of the
Yukon with its interminable number of channels and islands. We reached
Koatlik, at the mouth of the river, on the 28th, and came to St. Michaels
on the afternoon of the 30th, meeting our old acquaintance, the southern
gale, outside.*

— Lt. Frederick Schwatka, 1883

MATT: When we began planning our summerlong canoe trip, we'd
intended to pull out on the banks of Emmonak, a Yup'ik village
that's the last stop on the Yukon River before its swirling currents
become part of the Bering Sea. But continuous storm systems from the
Bering Sea had pinned us down some 60 miles upriver. Frustrated as
we were, it was time to go back to our cabin in Fairbanks, retrieve our
belongings from storage, return to our working lives. But we had no clue
what was waiting for us.

MEGAN: Back home we discovered that we had been robbed. Worse yet,
we'd been betrayed by a friend—one who'd helped us move our things

*Land, sea, and sky blend as a storm blows
over the Bering Sea in the Yukon River Delta.*

115

into storage for the summer. Gone were all of Matt's outdoor gear, some photographs, and his social security number. Sorting out the identity theft would take years. We also found that our quiet, cozy cabin had been trashed by the people we'd allowed to stay there. For five days we worked to get our lives back in order, and just as we were feeling more settled, the calendar read September 11, 2001. Terror attacks sent shock waves across the world, and our summer on the river quickly became a distant memory.

For weeks we questioned why we ever took the river trip, then we got Matt's film back from the lab in Anchorage. Just looking at the beautiful images renewed

Five-year-old Crystal Bird plays with her carved toy boat in the Yukon River village of Emmonak. She is wearing the traditional cotton kuspuk favored by many women.

our spirits and our faith in people. I remembered many days when I wanted to get off the river, but there was always somebody along the way to help us along. I began looking for people like that here.

MATT: The next summer, I returned to the delta, intent on seeing what we'd missed the previous year—the "rest of the story," so to speak. Unfortunately, Meg was unable to join me. It seemed odd to finish the trip without her.

I flew by small plane to Emmonak, a village of plywood shacks with industrial aluminum siding surrounded by thousands of sloughs. From the air, the town neatly lines the middle channel of the immense delta in western Alaska. Settling before historical record, the people here have enjoyed a plentiful bounty from the expansive flats. Seals, beluga whales, and three species of salmon are taken from the river. Millions of shorebirds, ducks, and geese pass through these wetlands. Add in the occasional moose or caribou and you have Alaska's version of a walk-in freezer. It is this land of plenty that drew the ancient Yup'ik to this spot, and that is what keeps most here today.

I struck a deal with a local man named Joey Lamont: he'd show me around the delta by boat and I'd fill up his gas tank. It was just over 10 miles from the village to the great river's mouth. Around the final bend, the last scraps of land were lost on the horizon, between gray sea and gray sky. I saw the end of Alaska—the map suddenly stops somewhere out in the distance, a territory that villagers call "blue water." Humps of mud peaked out above the surface and even more sat just inches underwater. Finding the main channel can be tricky even for the experienced.

Gingerly, we maneuvered through the shallows to a cutbank, and a pair of swans took flight across the river. I disembarked into the mud and grass that makes up the entire Yukon River Delta. Scoured smooth by eons of continual flooding, the smallest bump shows on the skyline. The grass hissed off my pants as I trudged to an enormous stump that had been carried from thousands of miles upriver. I climbed onto the weathered platform for a better view. For the moment, I was the highest point in the entire delta.

MEGAN: Not long after our return to Fairbanks, I was offered a job at a television station in Anchorage. Our wedding plans were in full swing, with the date just a

month away. It seemed like a stressful time to pick up and leave, but Matt and I agreed that a fresh start might do us some good. It was midwinter and −21°F when we married in a tiny rustic church at Arctic Circle Hot Springs Lodge, about 30 miles north of the Arctic Circle and the Yukon River. We shared our vows in a ceremony lit by lanterns and warmed with two wood-burning stoves. At the reception, a bluegrass band played music into the next morning.

The Yup'ik village of Emmonak is situated on Kwiguk Pass, a main channel in the Yukon River Delta. The community draws from resources on the Yukon River as well as the Bering Sea.

MATT: We'll always remember our summer on the Yukon, our days with *Lucille*, and the frustration of the unfinished journey. Reviewing the events of the intervening months seems like watching a movie in fast-forward. But it's an entertaining movie. Through good and bad times alike, we've endured and grown closer. Standing at the mouth of the Yukon River, I think to myself, *I wish Meg could see this*, knowing, as we both do, that the Yukon has staked a place in our hearts, and we'll be back.

BIBLIOGRAPHY

BOOKS

The Alaska Almanac, Facts About Alaska, 26th Edition. Portland: Alaska Northwest Books, 2002.

Orth, Donald J. *Dictionary of Alaska Place Names.* Geological Survey Professional Paper 567. Washington, D.C.: U.S. Government Printing Office, 1967, reprinted 1971.

Littlepage, Dean, and Gerri Dick. *Yukon River Guide: A Journey Through Time: From Dawson City to Circle.* Anchorage: Alaska Natural History Association, 1998.

Murie, Margaret. *Two In The Far North.* New York: Alfred A. Knopf, Inc., 1962.

Pierre, Berton. *The Klondike Fever: The Life and Death of the Last Great Gold Rush.* New York: Carroll & Graf Publishers, 1985.

Rennick, Penny, ed. *Alaska Geographic, The Middle Yukon River, Vol. 17. No. 3.* Anchorage: The Alaska Geographic Society, 1990.

Rennick, Penny, ed. *Alaska Geographic, The Lower Yukon River, Vol. 17, No. 4.* Anchorage: The Alaska Geographic Society, 1991.

Rennick, Penny, ed. *Alaska Geographic, The Upper Yukon Basin, Vol. 14, No. 4.* Anchorage: The Alaska Geographic Society, 1987.

Rennick, Penny, ed. *Alaska Geographic, Yukon Territory, Vol. 25, No. 2.* Anchorage: The Alaska Geographic Society, 1998.

Rourke, Mike. *Yukon River: Dawson City to Circle.* Houston, B.C.: Rivers North Publications, 1996.

Rourke, Mike. *Yukon River: Marsh Lake to Dawson City.* Houston, B.C.: Rivers North Publications, 1997.

WEB SITES

www.commerce.state.ak.us

www.virtualmuseum.ca

www.nps.gov/akso

www.pc.gc.ca

www.parkscanada.ca

On the beach, Pitkas Point, Alaska.